TRUTH IS OUR MASK

An Essay on Theological Method

William Lloyd Newell

UNIVERSITY
PRESS OF
AMERICA

Lanham • New York • London

Copyright © 1990 by

University Press of America,® Inc.

4720 Boston Way
Lanham, MD 20706

3 Henrietta Street
London WC2E 8LU England

Printed in the United States of America

British Cataloging in Publication Information Available

Library of Congress Cataloging-in-Publication Data

Newell, William Lloyd.
Truth is our mask : an essay on theological method /
by William Lloyd Newell.
p.   cm.
Includes bibliographical references.
1. Theology—Methodology.   2. Religions—Study and
teaching.   I. Title.
BR118.N49   1989   200'.72—dc20   89–39428 CIP

ISBN 0–8191–7620–6 (alk. paper)
ISBN 0–8191–7621–4 (pbk. : alk. paper)

The paper used in this publication meets the minimum requirements of American
National Standard for Information Sciences—Permanence of Paper for Printed Library
Materials, ANSI Z39.48–1984.   ∞

For my father

William Francis Newell

1903-1983

Whose only method was

life

TABLE OF CONTENTS

Introduction

When I was a boy I thought as a boy: baptized into my third naivete with the freeing waters of epoche, I began my tortuous assault on the redoubts of religious studies and theology without an assumption to my name. Feigned *tabula rasa* that I was, I was prelapsarian Adam about to seek the Mackintosh of the tree of knowledge: the transcendental unity undergirding the continental coils we call the major religions. But, alas, I have shed many tears in the loss of my matured innocence. The blush of critical knowledge has brought me through much pain to yet another naivete. I now trust my assumptions, the sovereign a prioris of my -- ready now -- Catholic youth. I smote prejudice hip and thigh and found among the detritus of assumptions past a friend: I discovered that I could trust them as a methodological tool in doing both religious studies and theology, whether it be religious study on this side of the continental divide or those of a more Eastern persuasion.

To my delight, I have jettisoned the search for the transcendent universal at the bottom of the religious heap since I now maintain that there are a prioris for each religion and possibly for each major segment of the human race; that the holy is radically different for each religion -- and *vivre la difference!* -- because the religions say that they are different, even if we faddish scholars want them to say that they are the same, underneath it all. Thus, I employ my a priori as a cognitive tool in doing the art and science of religion and theology in the knowledge that the a priori is the ontological and epistemological possibility of seeing and knowing anything at all. Oh, I know that prejudice can be a blind spot, but I also know that judgment, both the kind that serves as a prejudgment [a priori] and the kind that is subsequent to one's epistemological phantasm, is the efficient cause of knowledge: no judgment, no knowledge; no foreknowledge, then no data base against which to judge one's individual phantasmic experiences. The kind of prejudice that blinds one to the real cries out for the light of consciousness raising. One must have an implicit faith in the knowledge that such blind spots are repressions and, as I never tire of telling my students, repressions demand expression, and when the latter comes it is salutary, but messy. I believe in the inexorable thrust of the real, the stuff of truth, into our consciousness,thus changing prejudice from an organ of becalmed, numbed would be better, blindness into one of somewhat nervous cognition -- the apple from the Tree always sends us anxious into the bushes to hide our nakedness.

As you have probably discerned by now, one of my hobby horses is to be skeptical before the adoration we academics offer to the idol of objectivity. I don't think anyone is objective about anything, especially about religion. The object is to be understandingand fair. In this essay I intend to show that there are twin poles in our cognitive process, the interior and exterior; and that to hove to either side makes the results of our work lopsided. One cannot be so objective that he scotches out the very organ of thought. We aren't that capable of transcending our minds and what goes to make them up; we are, after all, subjects, not objects. Since the Renaissance we have been in reaction against authority, the subjectivity that binds reason to the holy before it can really unlimber itself. This reaction has skewed our method to the other side, to an authoritarian objectivity so humble that it refuses to allow the discursive as well as the non-discursiveside of our cognitive nature much room at all. That leaves one of our lobes, the mystical side, in a state of redundancy when one 'does' the mystical side of religion. Further, such objectivity in method forces us away from the continental shelves of our minds and hearts out onto a tiny spit of land that had its deed searched by the empirical method. Verification has narrowed us so that philosophy, theology and art became the fools of the university. One can no more positivisticallyverify the truth of Artistotle's Unmoved Mover than one can a Van Gogh painting. The transcendentals,the One, the True and the Good, as well as categories like Reality, became too ambitious for our philosophicalforebearslike Kant and Hume. But we are not only capable of much more truth than what we can quantify or replicate in a laboratory, we do that truth in myriads of ways every day. This essay seeks to begin to break us away from an imprisoning ontology and epistemology.Our cognitive innards know that they know and that they are essential components in the cognitive process. John Locke said all came through the phantasm, thus staying with Aristotle; but Locke also held to ontological [innate] knowledge of the self and God. We must be open to a method in religious studies and theology that includes the whole self. One that opens us up to an epistemology, ontology, aesthetics, philosophical and theological anthropology and psychology that is as cognitive as it is therapeutic; that is as open to empirical knowledge as to the forejudgmental knowledge in our a priori. Pure objectivity allows one too easily to evade the finite, the interior 'glop' of our humanity. As such, in theology as well as in religious studies, the empirical method becomes Manichean leaving us frightened of our bodies and fascinated with our minds and the purity of our souls. Such methodological Manicheanism reduces us to an Hegelian thrust towards our inner Godhead, the *imago dei*. But it makes us forget Paul's admonition that we are earthen vessels, mud pots holding the irrefragible God in our too terrible frailty. Method must include us as thinking and feeling animals, as whole humans. That is the contribution of depth psychology: to include the whole of us in 'doing' humanity and both the sacred sciences and the humanistic study of religions. We 'do' religious studies and theology with our bodies and minds. We work on our embodiments in symbol, rite and holy place. We look for the person in all of them and the encoded meaning implicit there so we can step back and derive, both for ourselves and those we serve, academically their meaning. The symbols are the myths and the *logoi* of the religions. They are the *loci* into which we and the gods pour themselves for our enrichment, our religious impoverishment and our academiclly salfivic perusal. The moments of describing the implicit and deriving the inferences encoded there offer us views of the salvific truths and how to go about enjoying them, respectively. But, these truths are so frequently to be found in the cracks of those earthen vessels, where we hurt and fear to go; where we are weak and possibly even evil. If Paul Ricoeur is correct, and I think that he is, in saying that our fragility [darkness] refracts our good, then it is precisely in raising this darkness to view that we even have the chance of seeing our inner truth and the outer truth obtruding in the pushy phantasms that fall our lot in knowing outer and inner realities.

And that is what this little book is about. It is a trek through the self as method. As such, it is not a complete method. Nothing is. It is a set of finger exercises revealing some of my thoughts after doing theology and religious studies since the early fifties, both as student and teacher. I hope to show how one's mind works and throw a small light on how to raise one's a prioris to view to see just how one sees and misses the persons one is studying in both one's own and other religions. I will demonstrate the hows and wherefores of method, outlining the moments I discern in method and some of the pitfalls I myself have observed from the bottom of the pit, and some I have seen my colleagues fall into. In a later companion volume I will apply the method and show how it works in a particular instance, i.e. when one works on Buddhist and Christian mysticism.

But, before I begin I would like to thank Dean Joseph Burke and Prof. Marilyn Smith, both of the College of Basic Studies of the University of Hartford, for their aid and encouragement in bringing this study to light. For their help, both financial and human I am grateful. For Mrs. Cecelia Roach-Mathieu, whose kindness, encouragement and sense of humor sustained me both in the writing and glitch-seeking of this manuscript. For my loving and wife, whose unstinting support and encouragement brought me through the Scylla and Charybdis of the book's parturition: *almae, amanti Lois; semper ridens effulgensque.* And lastly, for the many professors and students both here and abroad who posed the many problems that broke into my own prejudices showing me the *chiaroscuro* of them, I am eternally grateful. What light is here is, in large part, due to the questions they and the joys and pain of their lives posed for me. What errors and ignorance befall you in these pages, dear reader, is entirely mine. I hope both the light and the ignorance serve you in your own quest.

University of Hartford
Winter, the First Sunday
of Lent, 1989

Chapter I

Paradigms

I grew up in a mill town in Yankee Connecticut. Most of us were Catholic ethnics, so there were few Protestants to observe or by whom we Catholics could be observed. The few there were pretty much ran things from the senior workingmen's posts in the mills to the captains of industry who lived in houses far removed from our wooden two and three family framehouses. The rich ones sent their kids to schools most of us entered as servants, a few as students, but none as equals.

The good priests who schooled us told us that no one who knew history could be a Protestant; that history favored the "old Church" in its claims to primacy and exclusivity. The Protestant children I played with would occasionally tell me about the darker dalliances of priests and nuns; about graveyards for little things fathered by shadowy sacerdotal figures, placed there for the good of the Church and the peace of their bastardizing progenitors. We never knew how the babies died, but the inference was monial infanticide. The upshot was that we little Catholics and Protestants learned our faiths through prisms of religious mistrust.

But, like all things, there was another side to our lives, lived together in those smoky towns of my youth. We had school chums and neighbors who professed the Methodist or Baptist faith; good people who lived decent lives, even though they didn't seem as lively in their worship or pungent in their lifestyles as we were. (One of our "pols", in a waggish mood, said that they did not seem to sweat, meaning that they were cooler and duller than were we Irish, Italian, Polish and Lithuanian Americans, whose neighborhoods had churches and bars almost on every block).

So, even if our neighbors had the social status, we were told that we had the Apostolic Success-ion, valid priestly orders and the sacraments linking us umbilically to the deity. We were never really taught that Protestants were beyond the pale of salvation; they were only 'materially heretical', and practiced their Christianity (they were 'Christian', we were Catholic) in what we called 'invincible ignorance'. That was the door to heaven for these generations of good people who were fathered in the

1

faith -- so we thought -- not by Peter, but by Luther or Calvin. Baptism brought them into the fold, and so they were ad liminal Catholics, even if against their will.

Our faith had sacraments and hierarchs, fasting and monasteries, novenas and the Virgin; saints for every church and ethnic clan; and, above all, the Mass. We knew every moment of our day how to discern the spirits moving our hearts. We had laws and rules of thumb to see if we were right with God or wrong with him, following a proscribed road or the smooth, but narrow, path to salvation. Our mothers were not called to lives of virginal innocence as 'brides of Christ' in the convents on the hill, but all the same they still practiced little forms of mysticism daily by murmuring mantras on worn rosaries -- practicing yoga intuitively -- as they sussurously rehearsed prayer and meditation, fused by breath rhythms which peacefully altered their consciousness as it inserted them into the Mysteries of Christ's life.

The Catholic ideal was a life of consecrated, loving virginity, poverty and obedience following the advice -- not command -- of Jesus in the Scriptures, because it was supposed to be easier to attain salvation that way instead of tying oneself down to spouse, land and the vagaries of one's will. The older religious orders favored contemplation over action. The newer ones like the Jesuits and the female congregations modeled on their Ignatian mysticism of finding God in all things went into the world vigorously seeking him in the surds of the refuse or forgotten of the world. Seeing God in the physical and moral lepers they tended served to unite them with him in the Mystical Body of Christ, which was the Church. But whether one's call be to convent or the married state, the end product was the same: a mystical union with the Divine Spouse of the Soul.

Protestants loved the Bible , its roomy immediacies with God and the freedom of conscience their spirituality and churchmanship afforded. We Catholics loved the Church and the surety that its sacraments evoked divine succour in the momentous times of our lives and that its teaching and attendant disciplines were underwritten by God himself. We believed that we had it all and that they had only a part, though a salvific part -- we never emphasized the latter truth very much, however.

Thus, we tolerated and were tolerated in return. We respected, even loved, our neighbors who went to church less frequently than we did but who lived such good lives. We went to school or off to war with them; we married them, and called them darling or son or father or mother or friend. But the 'little church on the hill', or the great Congregational church on the green still remained a sober reminder that our Catholic faith had been remaindered by a world that had passed it by so long ago; if we could, indeed, admit that fact in moments of candor.

But we never really knew these brothers and sisters of the other Christian communions, nor did they us. We were different from one another. We shared the same God , and, in our daily lives we loved each other, but our catechised minds forced our ecclesial hearts to excommunicate one another from our churchly affections.

The most obvious thing about us was that we were different. We shaped our lives along different lines. The spiritualities of northern Europe made our Protestant brothers and sisters masters of the marketplace, specialists in the secular. God was master 'out there' and they were mandated by Genesis to be his vicegerents 'down here'. The Catholic mind -- spurred on by the *analogia entis* which dictated that we not only were his images, but that we were his children and shared his very life -- shaped the Catholic minds and countries of Latin Europe very differently. The Baroque spirit and its Jesuit spirituality evoked the presence of God everywhere forcing a diffidence towards the new knowledge in theology, politics and economics. This rushed my Catholic forebears backward into another age while the muscular spiritualities of the Evangelicals pushed them into suzerainty of what came to be called 'Modernity'. Different values, based on a divergent reading of the Scriptures changed the minds and hearts, the thinking and affectivity of the two streams of western Christianity. And along with the divergence went a distinct change in transcendence and the very ability to perceive it. The Protestant churches took a decidedly non-mystical attitude towards the world and their lives in it. Catholics became ever more mystically inclined and desirous of spreading out where they could; and they could not in the so-called developed countries of northern Europe.

So they pushed out into the missions as much out of impotence before their northern-tier brethren and sisters as out of zeal for the faith; as much out of genuine need to engage in commerce as the darker side of the acquisitive spirit. To be a Protestant or Catholic came to mean something very different. We saw things differently; we thought and felt differently; we prayed differently. And our formative processes,both in the home and the universities reflected these differences. We came to have different gifts, and the way we used them vectored our worlds off into different places where they took different shapes.

3

While we time-shared God, the theological way we interpreted him wasn't shared. Our theologies are different because our faiths are different in so many ways.

To form a Protestant in a Catholic way would engage him in a process that demanded that he think-feel -- both are cognitive functions, as I will outline below -- in a Catholic way in everything. No one 'does' economics or politics or theology in a mode different from his formative process. If it demands that one see things, for instance, as a Catholic would, then one will see commerce and theology with mystical overtones. The bottom line in commerce must be personal and not purely quantitative, if one practices what one has been taught. The Catholic spirit is a 'gathering one' in all fields of endeavor, whether it be commercial or intellectual. It is to find God in all things and not allow the binary split which a more purely secular approach demands. Protestant spirituality allows a bicameral approach. Man is the master of the secular and God of the divine. The twain is difficult to bring together since God is not seen so clearly out in the street. God is the God of the heart, found in the Bible, and the God of the eschatological Kingdom. But it is our duty to bring about this Kingdom and when God comes he will judge it and reign over it, after making the appropriate discontinuities allowing us to know that it was he, after all, who caused it in the first place. So there is a different way of living and thinking and feeling between the classic medieval Catholic spirit which perdures to this day and the spirit of Modernity called the Protestant Spirit.

So, if a Catholic were to do, for instance, theology in a Protestant school, he would be doing it the more easily in a way derived from that intellectual spirit rather than the spirit in which he was formed. We Catholics not only pray differently, we not only feel differently, we think differently from our Protestant brothers and sisters. To make the crossover completely demands that one become somewhat changed by that different thing that one is not, be it Protestant or Catholic.

Vatican II and the vast reforms it demanded of us indicate that we Catholics have finally imbibed deeply of the waters of modernity and have brought our minds and hearts to embrace the secular. Our universities manifest the change, not only in Europe, but especially here in the United States where the sons and daughters of the immigrants wish to be, not only doctors and lawyers, but also scholars of the first water. This demanded that we change, that we bring in contemporary methodologies and let them take us where they would, within the

4

reasoned confines of faith. Our economics and politics are different because of it. As a consequence, Catholics fall into two camps: either we are capitalist to the hilt or socialist, the two directions the secular sectors have taken. In religion we employ the methods of literary criticism on our sacred books and as well as the authoritative utterances of our mitered teachers. The results of Catholicism's late meeting with modernity have produced not only a renaissance in Catholic thought. They have produced an explosion in Rome. The first phase was repressive, ending with the condemnation of the Modernists at the beginning of this century. The second phase ended with the Second Vatican Council in the sixties when the church finally listened to the world and learned from it with pain but without schism. At present, we seem to have entered a reactionary phase in which repression supersedes reason, looking for the middle ground a synthesis would give us. We have been Protestantized in the best sense: we have sat at the feet of its best scholars and come away the better for it.

But there is a difficulty, to which I alluded above. Protestantism is instinct with a spirit still markedly different from that of Roman Catholicism. To be faithful to one's Catholicism it is necessary that one do theology and even the history of religions according to the way one is, the way one thinks-feels. To be anything else is to be 'other', not to be oneself and therefore not to be authentic.

This essay is not only about method, but about the way our spiritual formations shape us to 'do' theology or religious studies in a variety of ways. It is my thesis that when we are unencumbered by other considerations, like fads or the necessity to be 'with it', we Catholics come away with a different set of conclusions than do Protestants working on the same Christian or non-Christian phenomena. Otherwise, why are we in different communions? We Catholics 'see' certain things that Protestants don't and vice versa because of the way our a prioris have shaped us; and the greatest a priori of them all is the transcendent itself which shapes us and which we serve. The rest of the a prioris are the little, secondary, shapers of our cognitive and affective makeup.

I began these thoughts in 1969 while studying the history of religions at Harvard's Center for the Study of World Religions, then headed by the eminent Wilfred Cantwell Smith. Sitting at the feet of that Protestant gentleman, whose goodness and scholarliness had so impressed me, I heard him deliver himself of a telling lecture on Hinduism's desire to sacralize everything. Their rituals saw to it that everything was blessed by the deities, and even divinized up to a point. After the lecture I went up to him and said, "Professor, any Boston Roman Catholic could have taken you to his priest who would have taken out his *Rituale Romanum*, the book of blessings, to show you that we bless everything from boats to babies. You didn't have to go to Hinduism to find that." He merely looked at me with knowing eyes and said nothing. We, who had lived cheek by jowl in theological communalism since the Ecumenical Council still did not know each other.

At the Center, the method I was being taught was mostly phenomenological epoche in which one put one's cognitive and affective apparatus into neutral wherever there was a prejudice so that one's objectivity could be preserved. This allowed one to 'see' the phenomenon somewhat as it was seen by the practitioner of the other religion. But, if something so central to Catholicism could be missed that easily by someone who had grown up among us, then what of something as central to Indian religion as mysticism? What of its contemplative tradition, so essential to the Indian religious experience? Could someone from a religion that had largely dropped mysticism from its lexicon and spirituality for something which the more easily fused God and the world really 'see' Hinduism as it was? Could he let the sea run through his veins, becoming vulnerable to the other religion so much that it would change him in the process; or would his 'objectivity' prove to be a barrier to this so necessary part of the process of studying the religions of others? In other words, was it possible to miss the mystical heart of the Indian experience and see only its philosophical head? I began to think so, more and more, as I slowly read the writings of both Hindus and the western exegetes of that religion. Reading the latter, made me feel as if I were reading about secularized western religion in dhoti dress. Something was wrong here.

Certainly, our biases, or better, our prejudices, can limit our vision, thereby cutting us off from the phenomena we wish to see; but not from all phenomena. Suppose a prejudice is a good thing? Suppose it is our formation principle, shaping us to lines handed down by religion, culture and clan lore and to the lines set by the major figures of our lives and the hopes they inspire. Suppose God, good, man, woman, virtue, vice, life, death, love and hate, country and religion are shaped in us before we even become aware we are in a formation process. What then?

I have no intention of sending us back metaecumenically to an entrenched Roman Catholic salient over against Protestantism. In my own life, I have enjoyed not only the growth afforded by Vatican Council II

-- much of which stood on the shoulders of theological work done by Protestant scholars -- , but had long before it undergone a profound change towards Protestantism in general and Martin Luther in particular. While doing a thesis on Luther's doctrine of justification, I saw for the first time that Luther's ideas of grace and justification not only could be construed in a Roman Catholic sense, but that, in its earlier years, his thought expressed the essence of Catholic dogma on faith and grace. My vision thus changed, I perceived things about Protestantism and Protestants that altered my life appreciably in that my relations with them and with certain of their leaders opened me to truths and friendships which I cherish on my deepest level. And, sad to say, I had to conclude that some of the standard Catholic scholarship on Luther, for instance Grisar's, was biased in the worst sense of that word. Thus, I am not saying that "Some of my best friends are Protestants..." or any such canard; I am saying that I have been changed profoundly by Protestant theology, by the Protestant vision of God and the Church. I am a better man for that; they have enriched me and my Catholicism. Yet, I remain Catholic. True ecumenism doesn't cause the loss of one's faith but causes the painful epiphanies both demanding and allowing it to grow.

Moreover, I still see that we are different; that our visions of our own faith as well as the faith of others are culture-specific and dogma-specific; i.e. not only do we tend to read our own faith and its manifestations into that of Hindus and Buddhists, but we -- by dint of the limiting factors of our faith vision -- are precluded from seeing certain aspects not only of those other faiths, but even of our own. We don't see what we believe, we see because we believe. One of the things Protestants miss, I submit, is the mystical element in most faiths, especially in Roman Catholicism, Hinduism and Buddhism. There is a history here; one which I shall give in outline form. Our present mindset is that of modernity and post-modernity. These are specific terms; and this is what I mean by them.

I

The unwritten and unwitting assumptions of our mindsets are broken down into three periods by Huston Smith in his *Beyond the Post-Modern Mind*: namely, the traditional Christian mindset, the modern and finally, the post-modern mind. The Christian mindset lasted until the time of the Reformation, which would make it the sixteenth century. It assumes that reality is personal, focusing on both God and the human person. As for the laws of nature, these were considered beyond our ken in pre-modern Christianity. Thus, salvation consisted, not in mastering the world and its mechanics, but in following the will of God manifested in the Commandments and laws of the Church. These assumptions were superseded by the onset of the modern era at the time of the Reformation. Modernity assumed, first, that reality **might** be personal, but that the order of reality is more important than is person. Second, reason can discern the order found in the world. Third, human fulfillment consists in the discovery of and exploitation of these laws of nature uncovered by scientific methodologies. The postmodern mind, which originated in the last century, assumes that the world may not be ordered, or, if so, that it may be beyond our comprehension. Further, reality is not personal. (1) Thus we have shifted from a person-centered world and ethics to an impersonal one and the morality that implies

The modern mind mistrusts the higher planes of reality like God, the soul, good, nobility and even person. This mindset matured during the Enlightenment, which flourished much more in the Protestant north than in southern climes where Catholicism flourished. In fact, the intellectual leaders of the last four centuries have been by and large Protestant and secular, not Roman Catholic. Hence, if one wished either to learn or practice the wisdom of modernity one had to do so in a university which based its learning on the assumptions of modernity. Such a university might have been a totally secular institution or a Protestant one which more or less had to accept the new knowledge if it wished to be worthy of the name 'center of learning', or if it wished its graduates -- both cleric and lay -- to be attuned to the secularized realities of the workaday world. Hence, the chief difference which obtains between the old Catholic mind -- persisting to a great extent in large areas of the contemporary Church -- and modernity is that modernity has lost faith in transcendence.

Huston Smith says, further, that both the modern and post-modern minds are reductionistic. This makes everything something else -- religion is what it does and no more. Gertrude Stein said that a rose is a rose to counter the bald reductionism which would make of it a peace offering between arguing spouses, an ornament on a dining room table. Both these mindsets are Promethean in that they will to control people and things through knowledge of the laws that govern them. This desire for power makes their epistemological laws empiricist; i.e., how they wish to validate their findings to be sure that they truly know something is judged by what can be seen or measured or quantified. This makes the canon of one's faith empiricist as well; one judges one's faith exclusively on the basis of one's personal experience. Its epistemology is also mechanistic; i.e. , it explains everything in impersonal terms. If its epistemology is empiricist, it follows that its ontology is naturalistic. So the real is the material component of a thing or person. Whatever is not

8

material does not exist. Hence, the supernatural does not exist; or if it does, it does not count. But if one is empirical in validating one's knowledge and naturalistic in 'seeing' the real, it follows that one's ethics are humanistic. This means that people are the measure of what is right and wrong. (2) No authority principle such as revelation or pope, or, in a sense, even God, can tell an individual that this is right and that is wrong.

Huston Smith sets up a rather useful schema paralleling the post-modern and modern mindsets with the traditional Christian one. With the moderns, science is the way to truth; with the old Christians, it is Revelation which is the way. The moderns say that the real is the material in things and people; the Christians say that it is the supernatural or transcendent which is the most real. The efficient cause of all is evolution to the moderns but creation to the Christians. Where all this leads the moderns (the final cause of it all) is towards secular progress; but the goal for Christian remains salvation. (3)

Hence, the post-modern begins with what he wants; the Christian with what God wants for him and for the world. What is true is generated from these modernistic desires; the true is what will take us to our goal. This, in turn, demands that the real be quantifiable in us and in the world; i.e., with what can be controlled in a laboratory. All this makes their anthropology see man and woman as merely parts of nature. So it is nature, not God or transcendence, which makes us meaningful. But any epistemology which aims so relentlessly at control denies *in principio* the very possibility of transcendence. (4)

Such reductionism abandons the mind when it must explain something in terms of something else (and lesser) rather than in terms of itself; i.e., God and people are explained continuously and relentlessly in terms of something lower. For instance, evolution is a good description of where we came from and where we are going; but, as an explanation of it all, it is a failure. H. Smith says that the phrase natural selection is a tautology: the fittest comes out to mean 'that which survives'. Jacques Monod said that the cornerstone of modern science is "the systematic that true knowledge can be got at by interpreting phenomena in terms of... purpose." But in science there is no such thing as blind or pure chance. Chance in science is a number; in a system with a teleology, such as religion, chance is a happening whose cause is beyond this world of sighted measurement. But we post-Darwinians know now that so many changes were demanded in organisms simultaneously and independently that "The number of generations through which a large number of immediately disadvantageous variations would have had to persist to turn reptiles into birds, say... makes the notion of raw chance preposterous." (5) Arthur Koestler investigated evolution and Darwinianism and termed the Nobel laureate Jacques Monod's *Chance and Necessity* something akin to Custer's Last Stand. Both Smith and Koestler say evolution as scientific description is "a citadel in ruins." Smith adds, "Do biologists really want to take on issues like "creation", "divine guidance", and "divine design"? (6)

If the empiricism and mechanism of the modern and post-modern minds demand a world where there is no transcendence, it demands that one's meaning is limited severely to a partial view of the world. Men and women are locked in on themselves with nowhere to go if things go badly; and they invariably do. So, when Freud said that affirmative world views (transcendent ones where God, good and love go to make up one's meaning) are products of wishful thinking (projection), he explained away the very possibility of full, or even partial, happiness for us.

Hence, scientific knowledge is limited as to origin and as to what questions it will or can answer. Science verifies data with hypothesis, not facts. Therefore, its findings must be interpreted; i.e., they need an hermeneutics. Science is self-contained; it asks its questions and answers them on the basis of its self-chosen assumptions. A theistic religion takes its assumptions from outside, i.e., from what one knows from revelation. Religion was rightly challenged by science for allowing its opening to the outside to become limited by authoritarianism and parochialism; now it challenges the scientific community for succumbing to the same ills.

Faith puts us into the world by showing us how we came to be there; how we are to live there and where we are ultimately going. It deals with pain and shows the possibility for happiness both here and after death. Empiricism limits one by locking one into the closet of the world. The solution must come by allowing humanism to insert us both into the world and into religion; into the whence, how and where of it.

Wilfred Cantwell Smith, in his *Faith and Belief*, says that secularism, armed with its empirical ally, has so changed our sociology of knowledge and our epistemology that the word 'belief' has come to mean something that is not necessarily true. Faith is universally, essentially, and generically human; and it may be a religious openness to a God, or a humanistic openness to the goodness of things as they operate in philosophy and politics. (7) Belief, for Smith, is the conceptual device religion uses to articulate its vision. But belief and believe have so lost their conceptual links to truth that, to Smith, they are actually used by secularized Protestant theologians, who, themselves, have an antipathy to religion, to subvert religion. (8) The scientific model has so taken charge of the modern and post-modern intellectual apparatus that it is only what one can validate empirically which can gain acceptance in academic circles. Smith goes on to say that empiricism finds concepts like Truth and the Real as too ambitious; one cannot know them since they are too large. One can only know what one can validate. Hence one can only know what one knows. Thus limited, one cannot know God; one can only believe him, or believe in him. (9) The paradigm which is our secular and cultural patrimony is an unwritten denial of both the transcendent and our capacity to know, and possibly experience, anything of it. When we are among our intellectual colleagues, we cannot articulate the transcendent whole; we can only stutter and lisp about its observable parts. The assumptions of the present day intellectual community are, according to Daniel Joseph Singal, that "man is a human animal"; that "the universe is inherently irrational"; that "morality is imbedded in history and not in immutable natural laws"; and that "personality is primarily determined by one's culture." (10)

There was a shift from the traditional Christian (Catholic) mindset to the modern one; and there is another shift aborning from the modern to the postmodern. Each of these shifts is from one major problem-solving model (paradigm) to another. Thomas S. Kuhn says that out of date science is not necessarily wrong; it is merely discarded. It is not necessarily wrong, since any and all paradigms are arbitrary boxes into which we force Nature so that we may have suitably scientific results. (11) The old church could not solve the problems of its day and so what came to be called the Enlightenment -- with its set of assumptions, already outlined -- took primacy of place in people's minds and hearts; and more the latter since one cleaves to one's assumptions as one does to a religious dogma: with zeal and perseverance.

Science and theology go in search of new tools with which to do the jobs at hand when the old won't work sufficiently well. Kuhn asserts that the new tools bespeak a wrenching break with the assumptions of the old; that science, and one would *a fortiori* conclude , theology, does not move forward in an incremental, but with a discontinual motion. It jumps by fits and starts, despite the smoothness in human scientific evolution that textbooks would portray. Kuhn defines a paradigm as a point of view powerful enough to overcome competing viewpoints and attract adherents, and open-ended enough to change in the future when new problems arise. (12) A paradigmatic viewpoint is a gathering of a variety of views into something cohesive. This, in turn, becomes a licensing agent for the young who would enter the field. These young people accept the view, untested, as an unarticulated assumption, an horizon, before which and within which they do their work. In this way, a paradigm not only solves problems, it provides its adherents with a language common to all and a tradition to be passed along in the university. This common ground and sameness of language minimize arguments among peers.

Those who share the old view do not count anymore. The paradigm which once drew the young into a community because its members found it useful in problem solving has lost its attraction. It cannot compete with the more cogent viewpoint. The old simply aren't listened to any more; they become unworthy of academic argumentation. (13) Kuhn asserts that scientists are no better than laypersons at articulating the assumptions by which they run their enterprise; neither are theologians, whose thought patterns run through the same processes. The last to be able to thematize the laws by which they operate are those licensed on the topmost levels of the various disciplines. Hence, when an empirical or theological method purports to operate from a so-called 'objective' stance, one free of a prioris, we must reject that claim as without foundation and discount it as not only a useless ideal, but one no longer worthy of academic discussion; we have gone beyond it to more cogent problem-solvers in both science and theology.

This is Kuhn's most daring assertion, and I fully agree with him: that science (and, I would add theology) runs by paradigms, not rules. The members of the community are expected to accept the assumptions without question. This paradigmatic group becomes a community through the agency of the paradigm itself. It not only solves problems; it serves to offer its adherents an identity. The community life practiced by one paradigmatic group is not that of another. They talk not with each other, but past each other. That is why they seem to come to no meaningful discourse; why they, at first sight, dislike each other. As it is in science, so is it in religion: one argues in a circular fashion, inferring *for* one's view *from* that same view. (14)

Paradigms may not be an articulated set of rules, but Kuhn concludes that they serve a normative function in the community. He maintains that the paradigm is constitutive of both science and nature. One can see because of one's paradigm; it is the enabling principle of the intellect, its *a priori* in philosophical and theological language, giving one the categories with which to see clearly, judge firmly and act prudently in the world.

Kuhn says that there is no such thing as neutral sensory experience -- and where does that put epoche? -- but that each of us is a prejudiced, i.e., not a neutral, observer of the outer and inner world. Nietzsche said the same thing more trenchantly by crying, "There is no such thing as an immaculate perception." A paradigm, therefore, is a set of expectations about how things are and will work. When things don't work in essential matters, the anomaly produces a crisis; and the crisis throws open the door for a new paradigm to arise. This happens no more peacefully in science than in religion. When our categories or masks no longer do the job our very identity is at stake, not just our intellectual schemata. Such impotence causes revolution, which is what the modern and post-modern mindsets reveal in our culture. (15)

Thus, without our paradigms -- which are our prejudices --, we cannot perceive anything in an organized, rational way. To throw them away in the euphoria afforded by epoche, is to leave ourselves naked; and Nietzsche says that everything deep must, perforce, remain hidden. Such objectivity is, therefore, impossible, not only in the empirical sciences, but especially in religion where interiority is the essence of the phenomenon. The epoche ideal demands that we throw away our masks, our eyes and hearts and wander blindly touching phenomena with our exposed nerve ends. One cannot come up with rational and fair conclusions here; one can only irritate the ganglia.

II

Therefore our vision is organized and in large part 'run' by our mindset; and our mindset has a history, be it traditional Christian (Roman Catholic or conservative Protestant), modern or post-modern. Much of our contemporary theology and history of religions have been heavily influenced by modernity and post-modernity. The Roman Church has been in reaction to this for centuries in an attempt to preserve its notion of the transcendent. Modernity broke out in large part as a reaction against the entrenched obscurantism of what was the Christian church of the day. Authority had become authoritarianism; revelation had become dogmatized; Christ had become clericalized; grace had become both a consumer item and something rather infantile in the way it was 'retailed' in the parish churches across Europe. Minds struggled to be free of the hard shell of mindless theology and its purveyors. An emerging middle class wanted its place in the economic and political sun; a place won by merit, not by noble birth or by dint of priestly ordination.

Hence a major shift in vision was in the offing; a paradigm shift of Olympian proportions. The modern mindset affected not only the emerging secular world, a world which was to control the political , economic and academic institutions from that day forth, but it was aided by the new, Protestant, theological paradigm which it had helped to emerge, just as it itself had been midwifed by the new theologians and their vision of God and the world. A new elite replaced the old 'Catholic' elite in the corridors of political and ecclesiastical power. What did this theological vision see; and what did it look like?

To limn out the vision of the new church one need only compare it with the general lines of the old one. Catholics value hierarchy. Their linkage with God is through a human agency prolonging the Incarnation; if it was the God-man who mediated God to us and commanded that other men be his vicars, the old church saw God's saving power working in those seminal contact points it called sacraments. Thus God's chosen salvific agency is the priesthood; a priesthood of the sole priest, Jesus Christ. It is he who acts when the liturgy is celebrated. The absolute saving power of God works, as it did with Christ, through Christ in the person of his ministers. Catholics saw the Petrine texts as underwriting the ministry which brought them their union with God. Peter was the Rock on which the Church was built and on which it had been sustained. Protestants saw a clergy in disarray. Erasmus said that one had only to walk down any alley in Amsterdam to be inundated with pleas from impoverished and demoralized clerics soliciting stipends for the celebration of Mass. Clerical incontinence was epidemic. Clerical ignorance was monumental, oppressing all classes, especially those emerging with the new knowledge afforded them by university training in Renaissance-affluent Europe. God had to be sought in a way which would not allow this clerical abomination to happen again. It was found by applying the new literary criticism to the Scriptures and finding a Church based on the simple lines of the nascent Church.

Where Catholics had placed a primacy on hierarchy, dogma, sacraments, and God's absolute power acting in and through them, Protestants valued the saving power of the revealed Word. The individual had an immediacy of contact with God, thus obviating the necessity of gaining access through the clergy, which now led a priesthood of all believers by breaking the bread of the Scriptural Christ for hearers in well-honed sermons. Less and less emphasis was placed on the Eucharistic

Word. It was the authority of the Scriptures held in the freedom of the individual versus the authority of the Church hierarchy over a free laity. The emphasis was critical. Clerical authority meant seeing God in a radically different way from the way the new communions saw him. The difference is critical to our study. The point of debate was on the doctrine of grace. In a word, Luther and Calvin held that God's absolute power (*potentia absoluta Dei*) worked extrinsically; i.e., grace did not work an interior change over men and women, but it rather covered them with the goodness of God. This was the way one was saved; and one had but to trust in God that this would be done -- the presence of the trust meant that God had already been there and saved one. It was faith alone (*fides sola*) and grace alone (*gratia sola*) which saved, not the well-wrought sacramental system of the Old Church which thought that this was the will of God.

The Old Church said that grace was intrinsic to our lives; that it changed us from within; that it wrought a mystical union with God that was so courageous on his part -- entering, as he did our darkest places -- so intense and loving, that it was like the sexual union between spouses. The mystical poetry of St. John of the Cross is replete with allusions to the spouse (*anima*= the soul, f.) held in loving union and thralldom by her heavenly Bridegroom. Thus mysticism was the ideal for the Roman Catholics of Luther's day, and it remains so to this day. Carl G. Jung, the son of a Calvinist minister, said that Protestantism destroyed its mystical base and its religious *mythos* when it construed II Corinthians 13:5, which maintains that God dwelled in us as he would in a house, to mean that God dwelled 'among' us, not 'in' us. Jung goes on to say that grace is not seen by Protestant theologians as residing in an individual, but in the collectivity of the Church; in the Church gathered for worship, not scattered. He cites Acts 17:28 , "For in him we live and move and have our being" as further proof that the original Protestant theologians falsified the myth and removed mysticism from their Church thereby. (16) Jung goes on to say that the Scriptures proclaim that we are gods: "I say that ye are Gods", says the psalmist; and Jesus quotes this to buttress what Jung, and the Old Church, saw as Jesus' own view of our relationship with God: namely, a mystical union. This is Jung on the Protestantism, in which he grew up, construing its classical position on grace.

This makes the union which Protestantism sees obtaining between God and humankind rather undifferentiated or atomized when compared with the intense personal and collective (Mystical Body of Christ concept, based on John and Paul) union Roman Catholics discern in the

15

Scriptures as constitutive of the Church itself. This vision differential makes the Roman Church somewhat feminine in Jung's view. It is referred to as a 'she', as mother, as bride. This makes for a sensuousness in both the Liturgy and Catholic life which is rather off-putting to Protestants, who prefer a more sober form of worship. The vestments of the old liturgy are rather rich and soft on a man. The music, the stained glass windows, the incense and chants conspire to weave an altered state of consciousness in the communicants that allows them to experience empirically the intense, joyous communion which is the 'Is' (existential situation) of the Church. This mystical union breaks out at times in the lives in the saints. St. Teresa of Avila swooned time and again when in the arms of her Divine Lover. Bernini's statue of the saint in ecstasy shows a woman looking very much like one in the arms of a human lover, a woman actually seeming to experience orgasm. Catholics mine the mystical and erotic figures of the Song of Songs to depict their relation with their loving Lord. I was in Rome when an American feminist theologian from New York was leading a group of her divinity students through a Roman Church. She fumed at the femininity of it all. She got the right perception, but missed the point. It is supposed to portray femininity: the Roman Catholic church is the bride of Christ mystically (really) united to him, being divinized by him.

The Catholic liturgy is based on a view of one's union which, when fitted out in brick and mortar, in art and the Order of Worship, makes the Protestant building and Liturgy seem distinctly sober and masculine over against Catholic sensuality and femininity. The spoken word has a primacy for the Protestants , both in its revealed and homiletic form. The preacher is not caparisoned in soft, colorful chasuble, but in a sober [frequently academic] robe. The focal point is not the table of mystical communion but the pulpit. We Catholics are, therefore, more on the Dionysiac side of things in our worship and style of life and this not only colors how we see God, but it is caused by that very ontological approach to him and happy union with him which causes the joy and sensuality in our lifestyle -- the dourness and blackness of many catholic countries is a counterpart to the autochthonous sensuality of those peoples in the first place. Protestants are , on the whole, more Appolonian because of their epistemological approach to God. Thus where the Catholics stress the *mythos* over logos, the Protestants reverse the process. The transcendent is thus not only experienced in a markedly different way, it may even be different as it is in the other religions. I have written elsewhere (17) that the most obvious thing about religions is that we are different; that we don't experience the same transcendent being in different ways, but that that Being is different and that it's wrong to falsify it by a facile ecumenism. If we would be ecumenical let us do it honestly so it will not prove ephemeral, the idyll of a bygone, happier, age. Thus we Catholics and Protestants not only see differently because we believe differently, but we are different and should do our theology and history of religions differently because our ontologies and epistemologies are in inverse proportion to each other, the primacy of the one causing the shape of the other. Where we Catholics see God in low descent united with us and uniting all humankind by walking with us in the streets -- a fact which often freezes us into contemplative inaction in secular matters -- Protestants see him still in high, non-analogical terms, allowing them much more freedom to get on with things in the world, shorn of the weight of an obscurantist clergy. We Catholics see God as a divine embolism within and Protestants see him as residing outside themselves. Our masks are our truths and we must not deny them lest we deny ourselves. To do religion in the same way without major changes would be to make the theologian schizoid, his faith over there and his methodology here. The good things about today's eirenicism is that where once the two communions diverged in fear and mutual loathing, they seem to converge today allowing the one to feed profitably and lovingly from the other.

Getting back to the history of our visions, that of Protestantism allowed the emerging middle class to subdue the world more than did our Catholic one. Protestantism's new mask allowed its adherents to see God's holy secularity . It construed the Incarnation in a healthy earthiness, which allowed the layperson to have direct access to God and the businessman and politician to employ their new knowledge in a way underwritten by the Scriptures themselves. The Catholics, in their turn, took their secularity in terms of art and a mystical spirituality. Michelangelo, Bernini and Leonardo da Vinci, Jesuit Baroque and the Baroque in general, praised God in a glorified man and woman. You never saw a more perfect figure of a man than Michelangelo's Moses; even his David pales before it. A sensuousness in art brought God to earth in a way consonant with the mystical vision Catholics had of themselves and of God and their Church. It was a joyous Church, yet there was the need to reform. There emerged renewed priests and nuns who called for penance within a context of a Church allied to art and mysticism. Protestants called for a life more in tune with the new science and its offspring, and emerging technology. Thus, life and brilliance and relevance passed the Catholics by except in art. Things were run in academia and the political-economic arena by men and women enjoying a view of things grounded much more in the Protestant vision than in the Roman Catholic one. The old church held on for dear life; the new church burgeoned along with the other child of modernity, secularity.

If the psychology of knowledge is correct in saying that one who views a thing changes the thing viewed, then what must one say of a Protestant viewing a mystical religion like Roman Catholicism, or like the Madhyamika Buddhism of Nagarjuna? Prescinding from the harshness which was the coinage Protestants and Catholics dealt in for almost four centuries, even the most irenic approach to either Catholicism or Buddhism from the Protestant side would miss much of what was going on mystically in the very effort to explain it to someone. According to quantum mechanics, there is no such thing as objectivity. One cannot eliminate oneself from the picture. Hence, to observe a thing changes it. (18)

I think that I have adequately outlined both the mindset and ideologies of modernity and postmodernity. Its Enlightenment fundamentalism, to borrow a phrase from Robert Bellah, has infused those licensed in the secular and divine sciences with the hubris that theirs is a superior position to traditional religion, which, for want of a better phrase, is Roman Catholicism in the West and the religions of the East elsewhere. And it is indeed true that the Church's position for the past several centuries has caused it to eschew the wisdoms and knowledge of modernity in order to hold onto other, more fundamental, values such as personalism and sacramental worship based on a rather more earthy interpretation of the Incarnation than is Protestantism's secular one. Both are founded on trust in God, but Protestantism in a way that puts God more distant than in Catholicism. God and the church are more invisible in the Protestant model. The Roman Church follows another scriptural model which allows its lines to be more visible and structured than does Protestantism, even though the present structure of the former is not totally based on the New Testament. The eschatological joy of God's mystical union with humankind had shaped the Church of Rome in a way that has kept it open to religions of a more traditional nature.

How frequently I have heard Muslims, Hindus, or Buddhists say that they can understand Catholics more easily than they can Protestants; and that Catholics are the ones they expect to understand them better than Protestants can. Why is this? Certainly not because we Catholics have been better equipped theologically in the past few centuries; the reverse is true. I believe it is due to our doctrine of grace, which is one of mystical union, and our tradition of contemplation, based on a more

18

obvious following of Jesus than is the more difficult state of 'being in the world' that the Protestants follow. The latter have chosen the more arduous road and done remarkably well with it. Their history is one of goodness and a rather hardy brand of Christianity; but they are not without critics within and without. The roots of their secularity were also those of the nation state, capitalism and a bourgeois ethos; not that Catholicism has been better in its practice of social justice. Some Latin American nations, now models of liberation theology, were, until recently, scandalous in their violation of human rights.

However, all in all, one rooted in Roman Catholicism is, I maintain, better equipped to 'see' certain things in Christianity and other, for instance, mystical religions such as Buddhism, because it is a sister mystical religion, replete with monks and nuns following lives of contemplation. Protestants can understand the roots of Buddhism, the Indian reform religion which wanted to do away with an arrogant and topheavy hierarchy and get at the root of things far better than Catholics. Protestants can understand the individual going it alone in and with God, following the 'inspiration' (conscience) within, the cognate of which, in Buddhism, is the force of one's Buddhanature. The freedom and simplicity of Buddhism gives the Protestant prejudice immediate access to that aspect of the religion. Buddhism's break with the Hindu bell, book and candle computes well with Protestantism's break with Roman liturgicism, except that Protestantism retained a heavy emphasis on the Book. But the heart of the Buddhist experience, both Theravada and the Mahayana, and especially the Madhyamika, is mysticism. That, I maintain, gives the religion that those steeped in another theology and spiritual tradition cannot have had. Except for German Pietists and some forms of American Protestants (especially the Pentecostals), Protestants have been wary of mysticism at best and hostile at worst. In all candor, this tends more or less heavily to distort their sensibility in so deep a way that their ability to 'see' the mysticism of a religion which is essentially one of mystical experience is blunted or finessed ab initio.

What happens so frequently is that such scholars become gratuitously bogged down in a rather meretricious Buddhist dialectics and mistake it for the heart of Buddhism. This is the howler I decry in so many western interpretations of Buddhism; and I find it very uncomfortable to see Buddhists from the Orient sitting by placidly while ham-handed western interpretations of their religion are fobbed off as the real thing when the feisty tradition of Buddhist dialectics should dictate that they defend themselves rather than hide behind their impeccable good manners. It is they, not we, who should say, "That's us!" But they

19

have been so heavily infected with the ideologies of western scholarship that they frequently seem incapable of knowing that they have been misinterpreted.

Thus, this essay is a modest set of methodological finger exercises showing how I think one can go about doing theology and religious studies methodologically. I will try to pull together an epistemology of my prejudices as not only the basis of my psychological identity but the cognitive factor pulling my heart and mind into position to draw meaning from both exterior and interior phenomena. Therefore, this is no more than an approach to method, but one which I hope might be of some help. It is a praxis first and a theoria second; in the doing do we find out who we are, and never fully so either, since we are not objects but subjects. Second, I hope it shows that if our way of doing religious studies differs due to our Catholic or Protestant mindsets, then our way of doing theology in our own traditions will give us differing readings of Christianity as well. This is because our prejudices differ so. Hence it is necessary for me to raise mine to view before going further.

III

These are my prejudices as best as I can thematize them. First, I have faith in God and in the Roman Catholic Church (and in all its sister Churches, in some way or other that I take new joy in but cannot yet fully understand). This means that I have an openness to the goodness of God and his work in history done first in Jesus Christ and continued vicariously in his name and power in the Church. This faith I interpret in a human way knowing that this is the way the knowledge of all things and people comes to us; i.e., by the way we relate to people and things.

This does not demand that at any time I put my mind and heart on hold: both are cognitive for me, since all knowledge is cognitive-emotive (the emotive teaches us no less deeply than does the intellect and is involved in every intellectual function we perform).

Second, I am not positivistic: I do not think that the only way to knowledge is through the natural sciences, which I consider essentially partial sciences and constitutionally unable to handle questions of human etiology, teleology and eschatology. But I am a humanist and use the humanities insofar as I am able in order to understand people and their secular and religious problems through their liberating influences -- and the one is the other in large measure, though not exclusively.

I am, therefore, privy to special knowledge through the agency of my church's revelation. But this knowledge is culture-specific, circumscribed by history's concreteness that both allows me to know and , at the same time, limits that knowledge. But I know, even in experiencing those limits in a most painful way, that what I know is bigger than I and greater than any statement can say. So, even in my critique, I am a hedger: if I honestly contradict the Church in a major dogma, I may have to publish it since I am a teacher, but I know that in time I am most likely to be proved partially right theologically, and wholly wrong religiously -- the distinction between the two is critical and only slowly learned through the plod of research and the weight of difficult experience.

Third, therefore, I distinguish between theology and religion. The symbol structure produced by the former rests on the latter as anterior and greater than it can ever be. Yet, there are times when I as theologian must go with inferences so as to be true to religion's originating intuitions.

Fourth, I value my and my contemporaries' knowledge as possibly the *loci* of revelation. Thus I am an empiricist, yet know that both I and all of us put together cannot be the repositories of all that the Church knows -- the church Whole is greater than the sum of its parts since it always transcends us. This means that we can be wrong, but that we have to value our experience, since the theology of the Church has most recently -- i.e. until the end of the last century -- taken it too lightly. Hence, God comes through our history, through our story. But he comes as well in those older stories recorded in our Scriptures and stories yet untold as well. So my empiricism is not final or conclusive in any of my historical or theological judgments; Revelation is, but where Revelation is shadowy, I claim freedom.

Fifth, I lay claim, therefore, to a certain relativity of knowledge on my part and on the part of official church statements, even dogmas. But when the Church has said "That's us" in a way that is dogma -- and it has not done so very often, creeds are rather brief and laconic affairs -- I defer to that judgment even when I have knowledge to the contrary; yet I am still bound to tell my peers what my knowledge to the contrary is in a spirit of fairness to my mind as well as to my Church since nothing can be insulted so deeply by hiding one's light under a bushel as one's own God-given intelligence.

Sixth, I know that my religious knowledge changes with my new findings and those of the humanities community; and I know that it changes when I open myself to the knowledge of other religious men and women.

Seventh, I abominate reductionism which holds that it can explain religion in terms of its functions or origins; but I do think that such critiques -- such as the reductionistic ones of Freud, Marx and Nietzsche -- have recovered much of value, like the rediscovery of man and woman principally because of their very limited, yet purified, visions (prejudices).

Eighth, I hold neither to a natural/supernatural nor to a body/soul dichotomy. This also demands the demolition of the three-tiered world of theologians and both a vertical and backward, reading of history. God is here now, in our history. He needs no super-language to speak and does not speak two languages, one to the body and another to the spirit. Such dichotomies can tell us much of value, as they have in a Hellenized theology; but they are in no way final in my view of things. Hence, my experience of the world is continuous with my experience of God; if he would become Incarnate, he puts off his ways and takes on ours without doing violence to either or creating anything more than he has already created in order to communicate with us. We can hear, see , speak and think quite well without the addition of supernatural or preternatural gifts. God's divine economy, where he is simplicity itself and abhors the otiose, defers to the laws of what he had once for all time ordained.

Ninth, I do not hold fully with the second law of thermodynamics -- neither did that most 'scientific' of men, Friedrich Engels. The world will not cool off and fall apart. Matter will be saved due to another irruption of God in the Last Days. Therefore my eschatology is much like that of the Protestant George Lindbeck. (19) His eschatology includes a personal relationship with God and one another and a personal faith response. But it relies most heavily on the remaking of heaven and earth, which the Hellenized theologies of the West demythologized , scotching out their images and symbols. Modern theology relies very heavily on the themes of remaking heaven and earth to interpret the "historical developmental" worldview. The work of men and women partakes of spiritual reality, so all matter and spirit, which are good of their nature, will partake of spirit eternally. God brings on the new age *ex abrupto* (disjunctively) by his own transcendent act. The world does not contain God and the new age of God, but it is the stuff out of which God makes his new world, even though the world will be remarkably changed in the process. So God guides whatever we do now in his name. The early church saw Greek philosophy as a *praeparatio evangelica* , and the new theology of the Roman Church, given official sanction in the decrees of the Second Vatican Council, sees human history and progress as one as well.

Hence, I see the world moving somewhat upward in evolutionary spirals. In all this I reflect Vatican Council II's theology in its *Decree on Religious Freedom, The Dogmatic Constitution on Divine Revelation,* in *The Dogmatic Constitution on the Church* and in *The Pastoral Constitution on the Church in the Modern World* (especially articles 5, 26 and 39 of the latter document). In this theology no one is seen as an independent holy Christian monad, but rather, each depends upon the other and each has an intrinsic dignity. There is need for human progress in the world, but one is warned in the document on modernity not to confuse this with God's Kingdom. Progress is vital, but not an exhaustive value for the Council teachers.

Tenth, my anthropology is this: unconditionality thematizes the human for us 20th century theologians and I am no different from them in this. This means that humankind takes its meaning from itself, not as symbol for something outside itself; as creature, humankind is substantive and needs no larger being to make sense. Man and woman have meaning without anything added to them, but the presence of evil indicates a deep flaw in humanity's magnificence, and the desire for more demands that More and cries out for it. What Marx, Freud and Nietzsche would call 'projection', that human needs 'create' gods, I would call a normal, human search for fulfillment, the fulfillment none of these three gave to our century with their magnificent humanism. Man and woman are unconditional, but not infinite, therefore. The experience of God is as man and woman, and in that experience of limitedness we find the ability to grow as person to the extent that we stretch in God. It is a parallax view of humankind: one sees the world through the rangefinder of human vision, yet the actual lens on reality is much deeper in us; it is the wisdom view of God given us in ever greater measures. Both views are true, but one is the Truth itself.

My theology and my hermeneutics are very much like that of contemporary Protestant theology. The Christian church went deeper and found God at the heart of human development, yet they left us autonomous in God; this means that we do not exist in a hierarchy that demands that we take our full meaning from being creatures. We take our meaning from being made in God's image; we take our pain from being creature, i.e. limited. The new theology made the first possible -- to be a human fully growing (Irenaeus' phrase runs: "God's glory is man alive") -- and the second bearable by placing both back in God. As Karl Rahner said, God is where we are; and wherever we are in truth and authenticity there is God.

Eleventh, I hold to the necessity of remythlogizing the Scriptures and religious language in general. *Logos* has held sway all too long -- for almost four centuries. *Mythos* tells us, through its power and through the power of criticism afforded by a rattling good critique of religion, about the transcendent within us. It tells us that both God and we are absolutes, since we are made in his image. We are absolute, though not infinite. *Mythos* allows us to redream the Gospel, to hear it preached fresh in our midst, without losing the knowledge and wisdom of religious language (the dogmas, theologies and official prayers) of the past.

Having said all this, I come to the critical twelfth point. I have studied and lived in a university and world atmosphere which has accepted too uncritically the modern and post-modern paradigms or visions of the world. These have told us about God , men and women and the things of the world in a very marvelous way. But they are very limited statements and have, themselves, become ideologies. A new synthesis is called for. I am painfully aware that my theology and Protestant theology are laden with the sometimes uncritical acceptance of these modern and post-modern ideologies. I am a man of my times. My theology is close to that of Protestantism in many points of central importance. But we are different, we Catholics and Protestants. Our theologies reflect our praxis and vice versa. The one flows from the other and , in turn, flows back into the other in a formative way. I am also aware of the common limits of Catholic and Protestant theology because I have only to advert to the history of both communions to recall our sad failures to love God and one another and to do the truth in love for the same reasons. I am also aware of my difference from Protestant historians of religion and from secularist phenomenologists in this sense: they look at mysticism from the outside. As a Catholic, I look at it from within. I believe this is a distinct and critical advantage for me.

I believe my intuition is correct that my Catholicism equips me to see and understand not only my faith but that of other people. And in particular, the mystically oriented Catholic faith allows me to view the mythos of the Incarnate Christ in a way different from the way Protestants see it. Method, as I see it, comes out one's way of reflecting theologically or religiously, out of one's grass roots faith made sophisticated by the rigors of a theological discipline. The rest of this essay will be a demonstration and a 'how to' for my intuition.

ENDNOTES: CHAPTER I

Paradigms

1. H. Smith, *Beyond the Post-Modern Mind*, New York, Crossroad, 1981, p. 6.
2. Ibid., pp. 77 f.
3. Ibid., p. 110.
4. Ibid, p. 134.
5. Ibid., pp. 171 ff.
6. Ibid., p. 173, cf. note 'e'.
7. Wilfred Cantwell Smith, *Faith and Belief*, Princeton, U. of Princeton Press, 1979, p. 129.
8. Ibid., p. 144.
9. Ibid., p. 147.
10. Singal in the New York Times review of his book *From Victorian To Modernist Thought in the South, 1919-1945*, N.Y. Times for 10-31-'82, p. 37.
11. Thomas S. Kuhn, *The Structure of Scientific Revolutions*, Chicago: U. of Chicago, 1962, pp. 2 f.
12. Ibid., pp. 6-10 passim.
13. Ibid., pp. 20-24 passim.
14. Ibid., p. 93.
15. Ibid., pp. 95, 97, 100, 108, 125 passim.
16. C.G. Jung, *Modern Psychology*, vols. 3&4, *The Process of Individuation: Three Eastern Texts and the Exercitia Spiritualia of St. Ignatius Loyola, Notes on Lectures given at the Eidgenossche Technische Hochschule, Zurich, OKT. 1938-1940*, not for publication, pp. 167 f.
17. Cf. my *Struggle and Submission: R.C. Zaehner on Mysticisms*, Washington: Univ. Press of America, 1981.
18. Gary Zukav, *The Dancing Wu Li Masters, an overview of the new physics*. New York: William Morrow, 1979, p. 56.
19. George A. Lindbeck, *The Future of Roman Catholic Theology*, London: S.P.C.K., 1970; Philadelphia: Fortress Press,1969, pp. 18 f.

Chapter II

The Virtue of Prejudice

Thus far we have seen that there are mindsets such as the Modern and Post-Modern, the Catholic and Protestant and that these have histories. Further, that such mindsets or paradigms are ways of viewing the world and that when one studies one does so to learn a paradigm. Paradigms or mindsets are formation devices and processes that tell us how to solve problems and which problems we can solve. They force nature into their box to produce results. They can be wrong, therefore, especially when faced with an anomaly. They tend to 'force' the anomalous data into their machine to grind out the same old answers to new problems. We are dealing with psychology and epistemology here; with how the mind works and how one can tell when one really knows the world outside and inside.

Now we move on to an intriguing set of problems. When Husserl's philosophy broke onto the world scene it set free many of our forebears. They could be totally open, presuppositionless, to 'see' what was out there. Phenomena were the determiners of the totally open mind. Then there was Sigmund Freud with his desire to do non-judgmental therapy; to face the patient without imposing his own categories on him or her so that he could deal with what was 'out there' in the patient. But both were wrong in their conclusions, even if they were correct and laudable in their motives. Modern science tells us that "the search for truth modifies truth". (1) This means that there is no sharp distinction between the subject and object, between the observer and the observed, between the phenomenologist and the phenomenon. The physicist N.R. Hanson says that not only are all data theory-laden but also that "all properties are observer-dependent."(2)

What does that mean for reality and our ability to know it? It has discredited what was called 'naive realism', the claim that there is a bedrock real 'out there' and that we can know it with full accuracy. Heisenberg's Uncertainty Principle , also known as the Principle of Indeterminacy, has given the lie to hubrised claims in science and any other discipline that the human mind can know all that there is to know about a thing. He learned that the greater the accuracy in determining the position of an electron the greater is the uncertainty with which one can measure its velocity. In other words, " the more accurately one of the quantities is known, the less accurately the other quantity is predictable". This means that to know one aspect of a thing with certainty means that another aspect of it, its other truth or truths, will not be known accurately. (3)

All this depends on the observer and the observed, on percepts, in other words. Matter is just not the hard stuff it was once thought to be. It is quite ethereal from the physicist's point of view -- and isn't that a cosmological-theological point of view these days? Teilhard de Chardin told us that the material stuff of the universe was moving towards the noosphere, the sphere of spirit and intelligibility. Hegel said it in his own way, too. And so did Friedrich Engels in his *Dialectics of Matter*; and I in my *Struggle and Submission*.

Thus the observer 'creates' reality, in a way; not that there is no real 'out there' or 'in here'. Aquinas solved that one for us with his theory of moderate realism. It's not as real as we think nor as ideal and unreal as we would like to think. In other words, there is truth to be known in us and in the extra-mental world. The empirical sciences, however, sent us religionists out into the world thinking we could think without prejudices: the fundamentalism of the Enlightenment lived on. As usual, the theologians were the last to catch on to the fad. When science was jettisoning it we were trumpeting it from our 'Div School' rostra. No wonder there was grass growing on the window sills of the Harvard Divinity School when Pusey took over the presidency of the university shortly after the Second World War.

What does all this mean? I submit that it indicates that one's interiority is the place for method to look today. We don't have to worry about objectivity and fairness. They will take care of themselves. What hasn't been taken care of is one's subjectivity. We don't approach 'reality' with anything resembling total openness. Foreknowledge and forejudgments form the very arena of our thinking and feeling apparatus; the Latin *prejudicium* covers both words for the simple fact that to judge beforehand includes to know beforehand; the greater includes the lesser. Our foreknowledge and forejudgments shape us, telling us what we see, like and dislike, want and don't want; telling us what is true and false, threatening and non-threatening. Telling us, in a word, what we can see and know and love and hate. No wonder Husserl and Freud wanted to get away from this cauldron of thoughts and feelings. But one cannot. Even today's therapists don't sit there, non-directively mumbling "Uh, huh.

28

Does that bother you?" anymore. (One had to study eight years to utter that phrase correctly or be drummed out of the academy.) Instead, today a therapist is just as likely to say, " For God's sake! don't do that, it's destructive and disgusting." One approaches one's patient with something akin to therapeutic and epistemological subjectivity, vetting what one hears with the canons of what is destructive and healthy in things mental. Times have changed, and we theologians and religious studies mavens should acknowledge it and do something about it. Many of us have done the first half, admitting that we must go at religion including our subjectivity. But how? The why and how of it is the stuff of this little book.

So, categories are back. Nietzsche freed us from them with his existentialism, saying that all the little seminarians at Tubingen were out shaking the bushes looking for them. Categories had atrophied us. Nietzsche helped cure us of the atrophy. But thought without structure is like a body without a skeleton, useless. We Catholics have categories by the bushel full. Aristotle gave them to us with his substance and the nine little accidents, and we have been adding accidents ever since. One can do worse than Aristotle. It gives one an anchor in the world so that one can derive some meaning from it. And one shouldn't scant that. But, one hasn't just the explicit categories with which to make methodological rules to follow as one does things theological. One has a set of sovereign and hidden assumptions, an implicit method which does much more than the explicit in shaping our thought and producing intellectual results. This inner realm of assumptions and cognitive devices I shall call the a priori. I know that this term has a history, so I will limit its meaning so as not to cause unnecessary confusion.

I

The A Priori

This part of the book is an ontology of the mind. That needn't frighten one off. All it means is that we intend to show what the mind can know. Thus, we are doing an anthropology, giving you our views on what the human person's mind is. My approach here is transcendental in the sense that it is universal and not particular, as other sciences are particular. Biology limits its object to the lower forms of life, zoology to the higher, etc. This aspect of method is not religious, since it is so universal. We are greater than our religions since they are particular and we are not. Their very effectiveness is to particularize us, to make us over in their image and likeness. Yet we transcend them every time we

29

question them, even though we believe them, believe *in* them and even love them.

The a priori is the transcendentals-- the One, The True and the Good -- or those universal and comprehensive categories which move us from ignorance to knowledge. (4) My method will use this aspect of Bernard Lonergan's thought, without assenting to his unproved assertion that the transcendent is the same in every culture and religion. He begs the question by restating it -- saying it is transcendent because it is transcendent says nothing. It is a tautology. It is like Karl Rahner's anonymous Christian: it allows the other no otherness, but, instead fashions him in one's own image and likeness. (One remembers Voltaire's quip about God here. God made us in his image and likeness and we returned the compliment.) I shall follow Rahner's concept of symbol and sign as essential to my view of method, but not his extrapolations about the transcendent. I have other views on that. When Lonergan says that the universal and comprehensive categories do not change with culture I must disagree. (5) They do. Not only the categories change somewhat, but the very transcendent changes. Anyone who has studied the religions knows that they are radically different. And that is because the transcendent is radically different in each one, not just that our perception of it is different. I believe R.C. Zaehner proved that with his huge corpus on the religions. They *may* be moving towards isomorphism, but that is yet to be seen. Ecumenism is not isomorphism: it accepts the otherness of the religiously different. Cognate does not mean identity.

Philosophically, we may define the a priori as the ontological capacity for thought. But, there is more to the a priori than that, than an ontology of the mind. The a priori must be seen psychologically, semantically and culturally as well as religiously.

As an ontological capacity for thought, the a priori is a power allowing one to process sense data and extrude from it universals, concepts drawn from its own innate or developed concepts. This power allows one to stretch out and go beyond where one is at present, to go where one is not, to overcome one's word poverty. As such, it is not just a cognitive capacity, it is therapeutic as well. Ernest Becker (6) said that the root of neurosis is word poverty, the inability to go out on the ice, beyond one's childhood formation, and explore new territory. Naming allows one to empower oneself in an anxiety situation. It allows one to change. So, the a priori is a transcendental power allowing one to universalize one's experience and put a name on it.

This is a dynamic function. But the a priori is also a residual power. Once things have been finalized, it dominates the capacity for perceiving, imposing on the new percepts the accepted, and now assumed and out of sight -- forgotten and therefore unknown -- view on the new. The old shapes the new, therefore, even to the point of domination. When H.G. Gadamer says that one is dominated by one's *Vorbegriffe* (foreknowledge or prejudice, or effective-history) without being aware of it he is saying philosophically what cognitive psychologists have validated empirically. (7) Something happens to one in one's formation process that shapes what one can and does see and know in the cognitive process. This means that concepts such as God, religion, country, mother, food, Republicans, dogs, baseball, etc. are a prioris or prejudices that tell us what we can like and dislike, what we can know or not know. This phase of the a prioristic activity produces concepts.

This moves us into the psychological aspect of the a priori or prejudice. Psychologically, the a priori is a race flux, somewhat like Jung's collective unconscious and Augustine's seeds. These are brought to fruition by one's life experience; by experience, then, through one's maternal-paternal and cultural formation. The power of those experiences delves down into our interiority demanding responses, which responses are the produces not so much ideas as preverbal thoughts, images and metaphors. As such, the psychological phase is under the domination of the imagination. This is where art and mysticism link up. They both bypass the discursive paradigms of our mind to get the subject linked up with the other subject in the text or religious artifact.

A brief digression is in order. With Heidegger, I hold that texts contain persons; that is, we either affirm or deny a text. It is not known and then judged, but judged as known, judged in relationship to one's existence. (8) (Every text, every church or temple is personal. Epoche told us not to get personal, but everything written or made religiously is personal. We seek the person inside the text, rite or building.) Hence understanding is always choice or decision. And the decision is made on the foreknowledge-forejudgment that forms one's cognitive process.

Even in nature mysticism the subject unites with world and its materiality -- including one's own -- as person. This is what the Greek Nous -- World Soul -- was trying to tell us without benefit of the distinctions Hebrew and Christian spiritual and philosophical psychology would make. There is something in us, on the bottom layer; psychologists call it the unconscious, the preconscious and the collective unconscious. It is a trove of percepts, a sack full of the seeds of the race and of our

31

humanity. Augustine's 'seeds' are the possibles of concepts and words that we may someday raise through the grammars of our paradigms to expression in word or gesture. This bottom layer, when united with interior or exterior matter , sees it somehow as personal, wrongly extrapolating from the overwhelming nature of the experience to see, for instance, a chair as an extension of the personal self. But rightly knowing that unity is always personal since we are persons. And we are material persons, we are bodies. Thus nature mysticism is always given in terms of person, and why not? When the Hindus speak of Atman they term it as that which is the substrate of the material universe, and the same in all. They didn't have the principle of individuation to work with, which allowed a racial a prioristic unity in us all, but disallowed the dissolution of the individual to safeguard the unity of the a priori which is a common datum of the best minds of our race. Thus, religion and art meet in the a priori. Both get to that level by bypassing the paradigms of the a prioristic families in which one lives to communicate discontinuities that fulfill our hopes, or to move one into totally new modalities. Paul and Muhammad are examples of the latter. The saints are examples of the former. Paul moved into a new religion. The saints are never the same since they have been seen and see face to face, have been loved and love heart to heart, have felt and known without intermediary. The dilation of mind and heart, of body as well, makes a new person, one not possible if paradigms had to be the gorgons at the door of the nether regions of the a priori. Thus, the a priori can change us by itself being changed by shortcircuiting the organizing principle of the mind, the paradigm.

II

The Paradigm

We have seen that the a priori has a preverbal, but concrete side. As such, it is an algebra for thought. Its reasoning is either instinctive or spontaneous; instinctive due to the power of so-called race consciousness implanted in it by the gene pool or by one's culture. When the a priori acts spontaneously it does so following rules -- spontaneous doesn't mean impulsive or without thought. It means that it does so quickly, following an explicit set of rules, learned in school to show one the way to concretely work with an object to produce what Lonergan calls "cumulative and progressive results." This aspect is the a priori filtering through as method. It is the mind working in a Kantian way bringing "the conditions of the possibility of knowing an object insofar as that knowledge is a priori." (9) But the implicit a priori is what is meant by

32

a paradigm. It is the person putting reasoning and feeling into words and metaphors, respectively. Then one begins to follow the rules of the game, though reality is a bit impoverished by the process. This is so since words cannot possibly get 'at' all the reality one sees or knows is there. Again, this is Heisenberg's principle of indeterminacy in action. Knowing one thing is to miss some of its counterpart.

What a paradigm becomes here is a semantic schema, telling the mind which word goes with which and in what order. It is a censor and a grammar, picking words and placing them according to implicit rules of order. What Kuhn has told us is that paradigms are rules, but unknown rules. What cognitive psychology tells us is that they are known but forgotten. This means that they are either forgotten because they are too painful and need to be repressed but active -- and Freud taught us that repression demands expression -- or because they have become so obvious that they serve as the transcendental horizon towards which the mind traverses its arcs towards the One, the True and the Good. This means that cognition is a product both of vigilance and inattention. The paradigm is always active, though, either as censor or attender. As censor, it filters out the painful from awareness, constantly scanning percepts for what is acceptable and unacceptable. This brings us to prejudice, or the a priori as bias. The filter is circuited into the part of the brain that cognizes. They shape what can be known, but they also know. (10)

What this means is that one's personal needs or the demands of one's community (religion, family, culture, etc.) tell one what can be known and with what words it can be said. This is the a priori as longterm memory become filter. As such, what is stored sorts and prepackages what comes to awareness. If too much information gets through one becomes anxious either because of sensory overload or due to the necessity of keeping oneself or one's community together. The wrong kind of knowledge (truth) hurts both the individual and the communities to which he belongs, whether culture, clan or religion. Therefore, an enormous amount of analysis happens before things get to awareness and find a place in the longterm memory. Before a percept gets to awareness the memory scans information for salience. When knowledge would harm the individual or his community one part of the individual's brain knows what to do: it makes a permanent blind spot which effectively knows what's going on but doesn't allow the individual to bring it to awareness. Hence, the mind can know without the awareness of what is known. (11)

The cognitive psychologist Daniel Goleman holds that much or most consequential activity in the mind goes on outside awareness, and is guided by well-learned sequences. This means that the process of sifting through information is largely preconscious, i.e. not available to consciousness or awareness. (12) He concludes that consciousness is not the rule, though it seems to be, but the exception; that 99.9% of cognition may be unconscious. An interesting experiment is to arrange on a blank sheet of paper a heavy X and a black dot about half an inch in diameter. Place them at the same height but about four inches apart. Now hold the paper at arm's length with your right hand and close your left eye. Then focus on the cross. Then draw the paper towards your eyes. You will notice that when the paper gets between ten to fifteen inches from your eyes the dot disappears. This is a physiological example of a blind spot. Goleman says that to him and his colleagues it means that what happens on the physiological level affects us intellectually. This means that we are programmed to see some things and not see others. The thing is, we don't know that the program is operative at all. It was placed there by the demands of one's personal or communitarian life.

The paradigm as semantic schematizer organizes our experience to give it meaning according to its grammar. It operates on assumptions or a theory of how experience works. These paradigms are inarticulated theories about events, constantly testing themselves against reality. (13) It is interesting to note that our psychological blind spots, placed there by repression, take in all the details but reject all the feeling content; they take the body but scotch out the soul. Such paradigms determine the very scope of our attention. (14) The most highly activated or charged schema dominates consciousness. Goleman concludes that the overwhelming weight of experimental evidence says that unconscious processing -- with its attendant acceptance and rejection of data -- goes on as he has stated. Therefore, "perception need not be conscious." The difficulty is that under ordinary circumstances we can never know what information the paradigms have filtered out. (15)

What directs the mind to block out this and accept that? Goleman says that lacunas are metaschemas creating blind spots by directing lesser paradigms to be diverted so that one won't look at what is forbidden. (16) The quintessential lacuna is repression. Freud says that repression happens when someone rejects something and keeps it out of consciousness. As such, the a priori as lacuna is a defense mechanism, a device for diverting attention from painful information. (17) This makes repression quite important in any study of theological method for the simple reason that it is such a subtle and powerful phenomenon that it is not just a forgetting of painful material, but more importantly, it is a forgetting that one has forgotten. When the mechanism is successful it becomes buried, part of one's a priori, an assumption that is sovereign yet unknown. This makes the paradigm as repressor a molder of style. Repression gives us a style of doing things. (18) When this style is wedded to person or groups it becomes their character. Wilhelm Reich says that character is an armor warding off anxieties. These paradigms create anxiety-free zones in which one becomes free to develop, to think and feel and mature his thought and character. They also create anxiety-laden zones, taboo areas in which one is not only not free to grow, one is not even free to know. Therefore by creating these anxiety-free or laden zones one has fashioned a way of knowing. The a priori as paradigm develops one's character. Goleman says it this way, that this style "is a mode of attending [which] is crucial to an entire way of being; that is, that cognition shapes character."

These cognitional styles shaped by one's paradigm have a range running from the normal to the neurotic. What we might term a hermeneutics of suspicion Goleman calls a paranoid style. He calls it the 'detective' mentality where one is suspicious of everything and accepts nothing at face value. This type misses the obvious in things because his attention is off, skewed in another direction. It is "attention guided by a lack of interest in the obvious." (20) I find this style in either many an overly secularized scholar or one from a mainline Protestant background doing mystical religions such as Hinduism or Buddhism. What comes out is frequently not exegesis but eisegesis. It looks more like a western phenomenon, like secular humanism or Protestantism than what it is. Catholics have fallen prey to the same morbidity when they fail to notice the obvious about Protestants, that they are Christian, that they share in the life of Christ and a valid ecclesial body. The Catholic mentality shapes one's paradigm to find an epiphany in a high magisterial statement, providing one with a link to the holy, to Christ or Peter. But the obvious is frequently not attended to: namely, is it reasonable, or is there something missing here? Is this an interim ethic made to soothe conservative or liberal clerics, and therefore reformable, or is it the straight truth? Lacunae seem to shape us all to some degree. Lacunae are the redaction critics of the soul, editing out what is painful and disallowed to proof the text of our conscious minds. The four gospels are proof of this. Four minds, four needs, four gospels.

This brings me to a very important point. I am not saying that the paradigm is only repressive, a device for the neurotic. I have used the findings of cognitive psychologists to highlight an epistemological point, one necessary for any study of method. The darker side of the paradigm is that it creates blind spots, ones which keep one from the truth of others. This might be totally necessary in one's situation, but it is not for everybody. The other side of the paradigm as schematizer is precisely seen in the four gospels. Four views of Jesus for four different constituencies. Four healthy views, seeing some things, consciously editing others, unconsciously editing others. The individual and the community have to edit to keep themselves on an even keel and stay together precisely as individuals and communities. Language, culture, religion, ethnic background all dictate what one will and can know. What one will know is limited by the necessities of language. The a priori cries out to be expressed. Language is a human necessity. We will be heard. But there is a *chiaroscuro* (light and dark side) to all this. As the preverbal concepts of the a priori struggle to be expressed, they pass through the semantic schemata posed by paradigms. The language fund, the grammars of that language, culture and clan impoverish every thought that hopes to get out. The best we can hope for is an approximation of our essence, never the whole. This is so since we are subjects, that means that our life is essentially immanent and strives to remain there even as it hopes to communicate. Thus we can never objectify ourselves, never fully examine our consciences, never get ourselves down on paper or in wood or stone. A symbol is a subject, an epiphany of one's interiority. Because it appears physically to oneself and the world that doesn't make it an object. Objects are impersonal. Symbols can never be impersonal. They are the sacraments of people, containing them in the way symbols do; the way metaphors contain hearts. Karl Rahner's *Foundations of Christian Faith* and his *Hearers of the Word* provide us with this aspect of anthropology. This is why literature suffers from so many noble, but failed, tries at portraying the human condition: we can never get ourselves down on paper. Later, I will give some thoughts on method as art and art as such. Suffice it to say, that attention must be focused. The a priori as preverbal conceptualizer is unfocused, unthematized. What is known is known but fuzzy. To thematize it, it becomes necessary to extrude it through the unforgiving orifices of language. Thus our soul is translated into words, and words create reality. But it is an impoverished reality because partial. We must have thoughts and they must have words, and words serve the grammars of our minds and cultures and religions, as well as our languages. This is the insight of modern liberalism. We are historical, culture-specific. When we utter the truth, it is true, but not all the truth we know, and not all the truth we can say, and, above all, not all the truth there is. Most of what we know, 99.99% of it eludes awareness. Unhappy person that we are, who shall deliver us from our sad estate? God as the final Word, limited, small, fraught with our sinfulness, yet not sinful; crucified yet risen. We must communicate, we must become words, but they are so...unfinal. That is the basis of the necessity of images, even divine ones. Our lacunae make idols of them, but there are true images abounding in the religions. That is what makes them tick: words.

This brings me to collective paradigms. If the a priori as paradigm, as linguistic schema and schematizer, shapes the mentality of individuals, it does so for those individuals joined in groups, whether those groups be as small as families or as large as churches or large ethnic segments of the human race. It is axiomatic that the visions out of which we create religions are revelations of truth and not illusions. When the foundational visions are gathered into the institutional grammars of what we call religion, these primers of the faiths become vital truths. They tell us the truth about Jesus or Yahweh, Allah or the Buddha. (There were to be no Scriptures in Buddhism, but the religious could not refrain. So, in a way, the Buddha became Sutra against his will. Religious people have an odd way of turning the tables on religious founders.) So truth becomes catechism, a teaching for the simple. And this teaching which came from on high bends back and forms the taught, just as any symbol does. We produce it and it returns the compliment. And these symbols direct our attention to certain things and away from other things, even if the latter be true. No religion can teach all the truth, they can contain it all, even as we Christians see Christ as the sacrament of God, equal to him. But though we can communicate the truth in its entirety, it is not a fully articulated truth since we can't hold it all intellectually or emotionally. To see the living God in all his splendor is too much, so we see the further side of God in our religions, as did Moses on the Mount. A religion, like any person, can contain all the truth but be aware of only a small portion of it at any given time. What the grammars (paradigms) of our faiths direct our attention to is the hard outlines of our vision. Thus we miss other truths even as we quest for and find the essentials of our faiths. It is Heisenberg's Principle of Indeterminacy in action. To get one truth is to be fuzzy about or miss another. It is the nature of the beast. This does not reduce us to some vapid relativism or syncretism. We still hold to the truths of our faiths as ultimate. But our grasp of them will always be proximate; apprehensive, not comprehensive. For Christians the ultimate rule of faith is the Bible, but the proximate one has always been conscience. And conscience is culture-specific, bound by history, clan, language, and -- sadly -- by fad.

What we see, our liberating and vital truths, can also become vital lies in our poor hands. It happens in this way. Our foundational religious visions perdure in our churches or religious communities becoming the collective mastic we call creeds. What happened sociologically and psychologically was that people synchronized their schemas to create religions. This allows the religious a communal method of interpreting events. The bonds of our communities are strengthened by our shared lights. But Erving Goffman demonstrates that they are also strengthened by shared blind spots. (21) These religious schemas become so much part of the fabric that they are communicated without being spoken of directly. In religion we tell people what is worth attending to and what is worthless or harmful. We sanction attention: "Don't entertain those thoughts or you will sin." Jesus said that one commits adultery in the heart, without even involving the body. Thus, power is communicated to religions to create a sociology of knowing rooted in the foundational schema and in the way the human founders of the religious structure set things up. Thus, when we ignore a truth in order to allay a fear, a shared defense, a lacuna or blind spot, is at work. Freud and Nietzsche saw that, given enough time, groups tend to become infantile. (22) Mircea Eliade said that they tend to rationalize first, then to become eccentric -- moving away from the central, foundational vision -- and then to become infantile. When this happens vital truths become vital lies. It makes those 'doing' theology or religious studies in those communities, whether they be churches, the secular academy or cultures, fall prey to buying into the hidden but sovereign style which we called paradigms. These collective paradigms license one in one's study. If one does not know how to go about doing one's discipline, then one does not get the required piece of paper that legitimates one as a member of the academy, whether that be a scientific or religious body. One does not question the paradigms -- Kuhn proved that -- since one isn't able to raise them to view. The proficient are the last ones to see what's going on. The maverick is better at it but draws lightening. (Vivre le gadfly!) It is so hard to say "Oh, yeah!" when everyone around you is saying "Amen!" That goes for all of us Ph.D.'s.

Thus all groups, religious included, tell us what we can think and how we can think it. It is amusing today to read of the chutzpa of our liberal forebears, breaking away from the suffocating authoritarianism of the Church in order to think without presuppositions, only to set up a new grammar of conventional wisdoms. Voltaire and Rousseau catechized us, and we of the universities sat in our lecture halls learning the new paradigms from our enlightened masters. Those masters were brilliant, but they were bound just as much as churchmen by the rules of psychology

38

and the sociology of knowledge. The social construction of reality created modernity and post-modernity from the ashes of Christendom. So, when Thomas S. Kuhn nailed his theses to the door of the new cathedrals of learning, our secularized universities, the secular magisterium howled its outrage. Credos in a quantum? Humbug! But he proved his point. We all think by focusing our thought and producing our words according to the grammars of our paradigms. Our a prioris, our prejudices, are constantly operative. It now becomes our task to know what part of our paradigm is known on the awareness level and what is known on the unconscious level. We will provide taxonomies of our personalities in chapter five, part of which deals with Jungian typology, but here it is well to dwell for a few moments on how groups develop shared paradigms, or thought and feeling patterns.

Goleman provides us with three axioms that limn out the dynamics of group paradigms. First, groups will think, feel and choose according to a pattern, repeating successes and failures, giving unanimity a higher value than accuracy. Second, most groups feel their views are not subjective, but reflect reality even when they don't. Logicians call this the fallacy of provincialism, being locked into a thought style without even knowing that it is but one among many ways of looking at reality. It is comforting to them to think that theirs is the only way to see things. In religions, we have seen that this made us say that ours is 'the' religion and another religion is 'a' religion. Third, from the family level up to the national or international religious level, groups organize paradigms of attention on when to be open and when to be closed to new situations. (23) One learns these patterns and they become lifestyles. I remember an American colleague who went to visit the main segment of his family, which had stayed at Calabria in Italy. The family welcomed the Professore with open arms, killing every chicken within reach and throwing a large feast for him. One of the young fathers had a two-year old hovering about his chair. When the meal was over he turned to my friend and said, "Watch this. Beppo, get mad, get really mad." The toddler stood up and clenched his fists and made his face turn red, aping how he had seen his father do it before him. Everyone laughed. But it throws into bold relief my contention that we learn how to think and feel from our groups. Of course, the primary group is the family. There we learn what to think, how to think; what to feel and how to feel. We learn whom to like and what to eat and what is good and what is bad. We even learn what to say and what can't be said. It comes down to this: the sum of shared schemas is the family's paradigm; it is unseen yet regulates what goes on every day in the mind and in family interactions. This may be applied to larger groups as nations, cultures and religions. The group's memory is manifested in its rituals since behavior is the "locus, the medium, the storage place of the paradigm as well as a means of expressing it and carrying out the plan it shapes." Thus families, cultures, nations and religions construct reality out of their shared schemas. The Scottish psychologist R.D. Laing says that families play a mind game called 'happy family'. Here, the family sanctions what may be said and how it is to be said and what may not be said. For instance, in a family a mother might forbid the family to say that Daddy is 'loaded' again. He is never loaded, he had 'headaches'. Laing provides us with a codification of just such a prohibited act: Rule A says, "Don't." Rule A1 says, " Rule A doesn't exist." Rule A2 says, "Don't discuss the existence or non-existence of rules A, A1 or A2. (24) This is an illustration of what Goleman calls Group Think, a pathology of a 'we' gone wrong. In this vein, Laing also offers what he calls his 'Knot'. It goes this way:

> The range of what we think and do
> is limited by what we fail to notice
> And because we fail to notice
> that we fail to notice
> there is little we can do
> to change
> until we notice
> how failing to notice
> shapes our thoughts and deeds. (25)

It might be naughty of me to say this, but I have observed that Roman Catholic Matrimonial Tribunals are granting divorces called annulments. I heartily agree with the compassion of the church granting this mercy as the classical 'second plank after shipwreck' to its penitents. But, even a casual phenomenology of what is going on reveals that it is a divorce. The defense is made that there never was a sacrament because one or both parties manifested a radical inability to form a *consortium vitae conjugalis*, the rubric of the Second Vatican Council which maintains that couples, to be married, must have a stable, mature and growing relationship (a *consortium vitae conjugalis*). The church says that it doesn't grant divorces since it has no divine sanction to do so. The Greek church does with its rubric of *Oikonomia*, Greek for good housekeeping, in which a couple is given a second chance at salvation after admitting it failed in a previous marriage. But the paradigm of the Roman Church is different. Its game of 'Happy Family' demands that the same thing be done, but be called an annulment, even after a marriage lasting years has been broken up. The church might well look to Galatians V where a phenomenology of the Holy Spirit's presence is offered. Where a couple manifests love, joy, peace, patience, kindness, generosity, fidelity, tolerance and self-control (St. Paul adds the salty reminder that "...no law exists against any of them.") it can only be of the Holy Spirit. Thus the church has begun slowly to amend its paradigm to allow the distinction to be made between ecclesiastical unworthiness to receive the sacrament and spiritual worthiness to receive them. In the external forum, it has set up rubrics to deal with real marriages that weren't spiritual in the sense of growing human relationships. It grants annulments to those who can prove this. To those who can't, but who manifest to themselves and a wise spiritual counsellor that they are spiritually worthy, an 'internal forum' solution is made allowing one to get back to the sacraments even though no piece of paper is forthcoming from the church to buttress their prudent discernment of the spirits. But, as yet, the church cannot say divorce, even though it gives them. *Operatio sequitur esse* -- a thing acts as it is. If it grants freedom it must have the power to do so. The trick is to find the right buzz words to act when the paradigm is breaking down and because anomalous situations can't be forced through them to produce the desired results. But the thing about paradigms is that they force data into their boxes -- their assumptions -- in order to produce results. The church has undergone paradigm shifts in its interpretation of scripture, allowing its scholars to use the methodologies of contemporary scholarship. It has allowed some of the tactics of existentialist ethics to find loopholes of mercy for those who find themselves in impossible situations and wish to remain in God. But it refuses existentialism as a theological strategy since it seems to go against its vision. Be that as it may, new paradigms are being born, but quietly. The church would rather that its mercy be offered those who don't fit into the right theological paradigms away from the limelight, but the academic community has been hassled, justifiably, by the married laity, to do something about it that will give them a piece of paper too. The creed demands that we believe in the church, and so people want that piece of paper since the church is the Mystical Body of Christ stretching out over space and time. Theological method today is a titanic struggle between paradigms. The present Pope, John Paul II, follows a paradigm in social justice that would shock most Catholic Americans, if they knew it. He is much farther to the left than mainstream American Christians. But in things sexual and where dogma and discipline are concerned he seems to follow a different theology, one that produces results much more like those of a previous age. Within individuals and groups, therefore, there may be a gaggle of paradigms, not one of which is paramount across the board. One should know which paradigm one follows on which questions and draw up a theological self-portrait. This is easier said than done, however.

Usually one finds out what one thinks while doing something rather than thinking about it. Praxis speaks louder than theoria in these matters.

Therefore, we notice *what* we notice without noticing *how* we notice. Transcendental method gives us an anthropology in this way: it highlights our capacity for knowledge even as it reveals it. Lonergan says that our quintessential transcendental ability is our penchant for asking questions: to ask one is to have transcended the problem in a way. Lest we think that the patterns exhibited by healthy or morbid paradigms are fixed, Goleman assures us that patterns are a dance of interacting parts. We have been trained to think that we are fixed in our thinking. We aren't.

It serves as a methodological *via negativa* to run down Goleman's thoughts on Group Think. Each group has a leader and must have one to provide structure and peace for the membership. In any group the constraints become quite subtle. In a family, a look or nod from the head or a sibling who has absorbed the family paradigm is sufficient to tell the offender that he has gone too far. The leader may inadvertently activate the group's constraints, which , in turn, inhibit the critical powers of those within the group. (26) Cardinal Newman knew that this would happen in the Roman communion when the First Vatican Council was considering defining papal infallibility. He said that people will stop thinking if what he considered an unripe doctrine was defined before it had time to mature. Shortly thereafter, the English Catholic Wilfred Ward said that nothing would make him happier with his morning tea and the Times of London than a daily infallible pronouncement. Within two generations the highly intelligent pope Pius XII, surrounded himself with brilliant German Jesuits from the Gregorian University as his resource people , and started grinding out a plethora of pronunciamenti. What it did to the Catholic theological community was to bring real independent growth to a halt since it had to spend all its time exegeting what the Holy Father meant. The critical powers of much of the church had atrophied and were only revived again with John XXIII's *aggiornamento,* a desire to update the church with a breath of secular fresh air.

The impetus for Group Think is to minimize anxiety and reinforce self-esteem. This causes groups to bend reality to fit the need. Group coziness rejects dissenting opinions threatening that coziness. The group truncates attention and information-gathering to meet the needs of that coziness and places unanimity over truth. Nietzsche said that the church didn't really want truth, and in this sense the mordant German was correct. The church or any group needs peace to produce results.

The church is not in business to run a university, but for the salvation of souls. This doesn't discount truth, the church is built on it. But its leaders are pastors, not theologians. Thus, leadership down through the years has stressed salvific truth over academic truth. This is one of the chief reasons for the rise of secular academia. It had to break away from the church in order to pursue the truths of the various disciplines. But academia has fallen into the same pattern of Group Think that was and is to be found in the churches. One conforms to the paradigms in order that things may be peaceful, or one suffers sanctions. In this wise the escutcheon of all groups might well be "Coziness Ueber Alles." It was a rubric followed by the Vatican that certain things were not to be said because they were "offensive to pious ears." Dostoevski's character the Grand Inquisitor, an eminent Spanish churchman, told a Christ returned to earth to get out of town since he was offending the coziness and peaceful structure the church had imposed. He might be right and holy, but the people were weak and the church leadership had to weigh values. Jesus lost out to group peace. One of the Fathers of the church said that if the truth scandalizes the people, give them the truth. His axiom wins when the church enters periods of openness and change. When it enters a time of retrenchment it tends to impose Group Think on its intellectuals and charismatic leaders. This sends a chill through academia and extending even into the business world. A French publishing house noted for providing some of the leading thinkers of the European church with a forum, leaders many of whom were silenced and then rehabilitated at the Vatican Council by becoming *periti* (experts) for bishops, has begun to refuse manuscripts that wouldn't be looked on favorably by church leadership. I am not indicting anyone, just citing a psychological dynamism. A Protestant pastor friend of mine said that the Who's Who of the leading thinkers of the clergy of his communion had left the ministry to get Ph.D.'s and teach. The lesson in all this is that pastoral life imposes constraints on one that force one to run at half speed so as not to shake up the people or the leadership. A splendid Catholic pastor once told me that if he taught his flock the full Gospel that he believed in they would hang him from the rafters. Therefore, leadership, whether it be mitered or doctored, imposes paradigmatic constraints on us all. It is well to be aware of that as one does one's intellectual work. Constraint is subtle and terrifies the soul, chilling its ardor for the truth. There is an essential difference between constraint and intellectual rigor.

The paradigm for Group Think runs this way. First, there is an *invulnerability illusion* where group euphoria inhibits thinking and criticism and assumes that anything the group undertakes will succeed. I remember a bishop going off to the Second Vatican Council, unwillingly, who said to his priests, "Why the Council? We have a winning team, why break it up?" His auxiliary bishop left the ministry within a few years after the Council due to frustration and the slow pace of change. Second, there is the *unanimity illusion.* This holds that once the group accepts a decision it must be right. It assumes consensus. Third, there is the phenomenon of *suppressed personal doubts* where dissenters impose censorship on themselves. The Second Vatican Council had to tell its leaders to express their doubts. A style of self-suppression had been imposed since they were altar boys since the church taught the truth. If one's thought wasn't isomorphic even to the very words of the theological formulae, one felt somewhat guilty and chose silence over dissent. This holds in a more subtle way in academia where the conventional wisdoms of a given paradigm become so powerful, where the pundits are so intellectually influential that dissent is pilloried and the dissenter publicly scorned in print. This is done with much more panache in European circles, where venting one's opinions is cultivated much more than it is here in America, where we are taught to be nice. It is difficult to swim against the stream.

Fourth, there are what Goleman calls *mindguards.* These scrutinize information so that it conforms to one's schema. It makes one pressure a dissenter to bring him into line. There is no zealot so pushy as one who is trying to save you from your thoughts. Fifth, *rationalization* keeps the group from considering any information that would devastate its positions. A bishop, newly appointed to a much larger see than he had ever ministered to, told his priests that they were the elite of the church. Then a Yale study of priests said that they were no better or worse psychologically than the normal run of Catholic laypersons. The number of resigned priests whose marriages have failed causes tongues to click and many to say that it was because they were in 'bad' marriages. The psychological truth is that priests are just normal people and half of normal Americans find their marriages ending in divorce. Group Think forces people to think otherwise, however. Sixth, there is an unstated assumption in the group's rightness which Goleman terms *ethical blindness.* Whether in academia, geopolitics or the church, one's family is assumed to be morally correct. How many Americans are shocked to find that our businessmen play fast and loose with the poor of the Third World; that our boys in Vietnam and our intelligence agents didn't play by the ethical rules; that we aren't as generous to the poor as, say, the Germans? Seventh, the group tends to think in stereotypes, positively or negatively misfocusing the lens through which they view another. This allows them to ignore painful information. It is easy to see the egregious injustices of South Africa. But to have lived in a country such as that allows one to see that the majority of South Africans are honest, hard-working Christians; that they are good and kind neighbors and not the rapacious louts we see on T.V. The reality is much more complex than the media allow. Change must come, but what then? It is Group Think to view those outside the group in dark tones and those inside in light ones, even when there is information available giving the lie to the group's view. (27)

Individuals find their identities within groups which share their paradigms or linguistic schemata. The sociologist Peter Berger says that language sets the parameters of life in any society giving meaning to both life in general and individual objects. Reality consists of acting with others who hold the same schemas. Meaning derives from frames, which Goleman defines as the shared definition of a situation organizing and governing our actions. For instance, frames tell us when we are involved in a game or when an event is sad, etc. As such, a frame is the public surface of collective schemas. In a word, frames tell us what is going on, thus defining the social order. (28) Society fails when our frames don't mesh with those of others in our society. In the sixties, American culture went into crisis when its young no longer accepted the economic and political goals their elders set for them. They found the work ethic and consumerism bourgeois. They rejected the assumption that Americans were morally superior to other nations, that what we do as a country will be right; and they protested against the Vietnam War. Catholics in the West rejected the accepted images of the Church as a 'perfect society' and went back for a more biblical one, preferring to term the church a pilgrim community, God's sinful children on the move towards being Christian. A static classical view was jettisoned and a dynamic modern one with historical consciousness was accepted. Personalism replaced an impersonal, category-weighted,theology in morality and spirituality. These new categories provided frames telling us what was going on, and the two camps -- old Church and new Church -- came up with, and continue to do so, differing interpretations of reality. One constructs reality, therefore, with one's paradigms and the frames in which one puts the language that the paradigm produces and allows. The old frames, like old paradigms, were put to pasture when they could not be put to new uses; when human misery couldn't be assuaged, when God could not be found in situations that -- when forced into the Procrustean boxes of older paradigms -- were not to be found in the ready-made theologies of the schools.

45

We know that we are dealing with a lacuna by the questions that we cannot ask as individuals or as a group. (29) Many Catholics don't dare disagree with a pope, Protestants don't handle the very existence of a pope very well. Catholics are learning to cope with the secular, but Protestants have trouble dealing with the sacramental. Catholics handle Christology in a much more worldly and incarnational way than do Protestants; the very existence notion of priesthood is a question Protestants don't like to handle. Ministry will do fine, thank you. In public;, Catholic bishops blush at the public mention of artificial birth control. Privately, it may well be another matter, and frequently is. In a word, the questions we won't handle or only tackle with great reluctance reveal our blind spots and demand to be looked at. We Catholics had to handle many very painful questions in going to the great universities of the world and being confronted with new paradigms. The Second Vatican Council legitimated many of our hard-earned findings, bringing into the paradigm and its frames new words with which to empower ourselves. New meaning came from these new frames.

After having said all these things about the bugbears of our blind spots, what do we do about them? Do we abandon our interiority and go into things without our foreknowledge and prejudices (a prioris) and their paradigms? Not at all. Goleman's conclusions (30) would advocate this strategy. But all he has done after having done such good work, is reveal his own blind spots in particular and the conventional methodological wisdoms of many in his university (sad to say, Harvard) in general: go into things without your prejudices in place, put things into neutral, don't judge so that you can see what is there. Nonsense! use them so that you can see. That's the very point. Our a prioris and our paradigms allow us to see. The a priori is an ontological capacity for thought. Put it into neutral and you have a mind running without going anywhere. An old theological saw has it that *abusum non tollit usum* -- abuse mustn't foreclose the healthy possibility of use. I hew to that line. Again, there is the specter of the Manichee here in this Enlightenment elitism. We are frightened of our blindness so we refuse to see what we can see. If we Catholics can change, anyone can. And we have done so without schism and without the other catastrophes predicted by the 'prophets of doom' who surrounded Pope John XXIII before the Council. And he was an old conservative in his eighties. He just couldn't stand seeing people suffer needlessly because we refused to give up theological paradigms that didn't work anymore. (And I hope we don't canonize the holy old man. If we do we'll lose him in the glitzy hagiographies which are sure to follow.)

Freud said that the analyst was to open his conscious level in an unfocused way to the patient since focus concentrates attention and causes us to lose the full play of truth and feeling content. That's just fallacious. An unfocused brain must become focused as it passes from the preconscious a priori level through the paradigms. Language creates the reality in therapy as in all things. It creates it in theology as well. We must be prepared to fail, to delve into our dark spots in order to get to the light. To do other is to fear the human body and frailty as did the Manichees of old and the modern elitist ones who claim truth as their particular preserve. I agree with Freud and Goleman that the trick is to get to the other's a priori, be that other a patient or a religion which we are studying. Heart must speak with immediacy to heart, mind to mind -- and both are fused in the human, we have felt-knowns, nothing else, and certainly nothing more. But coming back through the other's paradigms we have to use our language to understand his. Certainly, we will learn his language, but only by beginning with our own and allowing it to fall by the wayside as we take on the other soul of another language; and each new person , each other person, is a language unto him- or herself. Yes, we must allow the other to remain other, but not at the expense of losing ourselves, which is what I saw people doing by following epoche and a faulty epistemology in which objectivity scotched their cognitive faculties out of the picture too much. I've witnessed mental crackups in highly trained scholars who allowed their emotive and religious lives to go one way while their minds went where their 'objective' methods dictated.

One scholar at Harvard said that he kept sane by living his religion through his pious wife; that way he could follow his craft and not let his interiority get in the way intellectually or emotionally. Method thrusts us into another's or even our own religion to bring heart to heart, the individual's a priori to that of the object of study. We always look for the other person in the thing studied. The undifferentiated a priori is the level of art, mysticism and all cognition, be it discursive or intuitive, religious or non-religious. I contend that not everybody can 'do' theology, no matter how intelligent, no matter how much he or she has studied, or where or with whom. One either has the *habitus theologicus*, the ability to feel-think theologically, or one doesn't. One cannot teach method, one does it. It is like hitting a baseball: either one has it or one doesn't. So then, why this book, you should be saying , dear reader? This book is for those who want to know how it is done in an intellectual way, even if they will never do it in a professional and magisterial way. It is also for those who have the charism of doing theology or religious studies and want to avoid some of the pitfalls. The rest of the chapters in this book will deal with the do's and don'ts I have run into in studying religion over the last thirty six years.

A last word on epoche. We honor it, but no one does it. Every mind is judgmental because of our transcendental nature, which is to have a mind horizoned with foreknowledge and forejudgments, and all knowledge is a product of judgments. It is these that pull us out into the deep, constantly asking why, persistently seeking unity, goodness and truth, looking for the More because there is so much of the less in their lives and it's just too painful to bear since their know they are meant for more than they get. We know that we are gods, so we seek God at the level of what Rahner calls our original affirmation. I would prefer to call it our originating affirmation. It is the Yes! God uttered when ha manned and womaned us in our mother's wombs. It is the soaring unifying good that is our truth and demands to be revealed even as it eludes it and tries to be coy. That which is most hidden demands to be revealed, and yet will not come forth directly and fully. We are subjects and can never be objectified *totaliter*. That is our mystery. In unraveling our own religion and that of others, therefore, we are unraveling ourselves, since all knowledge is self-knowledge. Our blind spots will tell us something about ourselves. They are a methodological *via negativa*. Our illuminating spots are our *via positiva*. Our epiphanies are our kataphatic ways to the truth -- those which are revealed through symbols. Our darknesses are our apophatic revelations, obscure but infallible ways to the mystery held by our a prioris; through a cloud of unknowing, which is a mystical, immediate knowledge that rebels at all discursive symbolization, but is to be found luxuriant in art.

Therefore, the a priori as a preconscious organ of intellection is an unconscious method, a natural --unlearned-- way to know. As paradigm, it becomes word. And as word it must follow grammars, albeit ones largely unknown to itself. The final epiphany is the way we manifest what we know, as word, discursively or as art. The words and artistic creations are both an illumination and a veiling of our truth. This is a mask, our mask.

Endnotes for Chapter II

The Virtue of Prejudice

1. Ian G. Barbour, *Issues in Science and Religion*. New York: Harper & Row, 1966, p. 285.
2. Ibid., note 8.
3. Ibid., p. 279.
4. Bernard Lonergan, *Method in Theology*. New York: Herder and Herder, 1972, p. 11.
5. Ibid.
6. Ernest Becker, *The Revolution in Psychiatry, The New Understanding of Man*. New York: The Free Press, 1974, p. 178.
7. Hans Georg Gadamer, *Truth and Method*. New York: Seabury Press, 1975, p. xxii.
8. I cannot locate this citation in Bultmann's works.
9. Lonergan, op. cit., xxiii.
10. Daniel Goleman, *Vital Lies, Simple Truths, the Psychology of Self-Deception*. New York: Simon and Schuster, 1958, p. 64.
11. Ibid., pp. 64f.
12. Ibid., p. 73.
13. Ibid., pp. 74-76 passim.
14. Ibid., p. 80.
15. Ibid., pp. 85, 90.
16. Ibid., pp. 106f.
17. Ibid., pp. 112f.
18. Ibid., p. 131.
19. Ibid., p. 134.
20. Ibid., p. 138.
21. Ibid., pp. 155f.
22. Ibid., pp. 58-61 passim.
23. Ibid., p. 169f.
24. Ibid., pp. 171-174.
25. Ibid., p. 24.
26. Ibid., p. 181.
27. Ibid., p. 183.
28. Ibid., pp. 197-209.
29. Ibid., PP. 228-233.
30. Ibid., p. 230.

CHAPTER III

Truth is Our Mask:
The A Priori Revealed

What we have seen thus far is that the a priori is a transcendental possibility of knowing, and that this makes it the home of the transcendent in us; that it thinks in a preverbal way on the deepest level, but that this deepest core which thinks and feels, better, feels-thinks, demands to express itself. This makes the next level of the a priori a paradigmatic one, a set of semantic schemata picking the right words and word patterns to go with the thought or intuition; and that it fashions these words according to the grammars of language, culture, ethnic background and religion. We know because our mind is constantly knowing, but most of what is known remains hidden from our awareness by blind spots and lacunae. Because of this, methodologists, following an Enlightenment fallacy, have determined that the best way to do any intellectual discipline was to be objective about it; to put one's prejudices away and get at the object without any presuppositions. But my contention is that we think with our presuppositions, that without them thought is impossible. Therefore method must include our a priori, be it Catholic, Protestant, secular humanist or atheist.

When we delve into ourselves, reaching for ways to express ourselves we begin to create reality. By this, I mean that the word 'reality' is an abstract noun. Knowledge is the product of abstraction from perception of the real and a universalization [naming] of that experience. The real is not abstract but reality is. So we know what we have partially created; we know only what we know, not the real *qua tale*. The real, both objective and subjective, are the polar imperatives challenging us to know and grow, teaching us by their bloodying ways to become human through knowing. Whenever we communicate we create symbols, masks through which we speak our hearts and minds; masks which, at the same time that they illuminate, obscure our hiddenmost reality not only from our auditor, but, and especially, from ourselves as well. Communication is a *chiaroscuro* dynamism.

In this light, method must be first construed and practiced as an art. The science of it is posterior to the art of thinking and communicating. Getting at ourselves is what we do when we study religions to make sense of them. All knowledge is primarily for ourselves. This is why most of us speak in soliloquies rather than dialogues. Dialogue means we give ourselves away, we die a bit each time we open ourselves up in that way. To admit that an other is really not just an extension of our needs is to admit the need to change to meet the requirements of becoming isomorphic with him for the time it requires to communicate. But such isomorphism changes us for good if it is real, authentic, and not just arbitrary. Thus, in this chapter, we shall see how our subjectivity comes to fruition in going out to the other; that it is an art. Then we shall do a systematics of symbol, how one knows when one is really communicating oneself to the other. One must communicate the self to know the self; then one must own what one has created through the language of words or the plastic arts.

I

Method as Art

In India man falls into the fate of his sin. In Islam he falls into the sin of his fate. In Judaism God gave commandments, not advice (1), but in the original religion of the Buddha the situation was the opposite: he merely advised his listeners, eschewing Command, Scripture and the entails of religion. He offered nothing like rite, prayer or a systematics of his vision. In the Buddhism of the second century C.E. Buddhist mystic Nagarjuna, when one experiences the vacuity of world, man, thought and sin he reconciles all opposites and achieves bliss. Nagarjuna, tried to cut away the accretions of four or five centuries of Buddhism in order to revive the religion of Gautama, the Buddha. He realized that Gautama made no claims to having had a revelation which must be written down and revered. Gautama did not become Book or God. He lived in an India redolent of religion (the country could hardly bear another) so he longed to erect none, and did not knowingly do so. He flowed with the stream of Indian religiosity. He did not even like philosophy, so he would not, and did not, impose that on his listeners either. He was not a messianic figure and preached no God exclusively. The stream of Indian life would amply take care of that. His only claim was to have been enlightened. He preached to that fact and advised others as to how they might achieve results commensurate with his own, but on their own terms. No one's enlightenment was like anyone else's. There is the rub: he made men and women their own paradigm and his disciples returned

51

the compliment. Advice became command; saying gave way to Sutra. Religious people have a way of reversing the tables. Calvin said that our mind is an idol factory, and he wasn't far off the mark.

Like the Buddha and the Mahayana mystic Nagarjuna after him, I am offering the reader advice , not commands,about how one **might** proceed methodologically. I cannot be apodictic about it, even though my system seems to work for me, methodological strategies stay pretty much fixed, though the tactics change rather radically, shifting like continental plates. Each one's method, however, must be unique to himself since the cognitive faculty is tied to the transcendent possibilities, that is to one's a prioris, and they are different from individual to individual, from group to group. Indians should do religious studies differently from the way Methodists do them. My method is also tied to my personality, which is intuitive and artistic. Thus my Roman Catholicism ties me to that particular view of religion and its transcendent reality and my peculiar nature is to do both history and theology intuitively. This may seem impossible to some and shallow to many. However Freud's critique of religion and the religious soul was just that: utterly and solely intuitive. He went to other disciplines to buttress his shatteringly accurate hunches, then and there did he fail, but not in his original hunches. Thus this study does offer a systematics, since not only my mind but all minds must offer an organizational scheme for our perceptions, but it rises or falls on my intuitions, both on method and when I get around to employing it on a theological issue.

The reader might well be saying at this point, "Then, if his thought is so idiosyncratic, why go on reading?" I will offer a systematics of the idiosyncratic, a rationale for tying my feeling-knowing (cognitive) faculty to the a prioristic transcendent peculiar both to my faith and to me as a practitioner of it. The value I foresee in this is that my insights may free others to allow them to tread their own unique path to the transcendent within; and the transcendent is by definition something that goes into one's being by pulling one beyond it to both the self as subject known as such and the other known in the same way. The transcendent always pushes one beyond where one would go to where it demands the truths be known, our own and that of other 'subjects'. But, as the Buddha said of those who set models for others, "If you see the Buddha, kill him." The same goes for my method. This is not false humility, nor am I shooting myself in the foot. Hence, at this stage I am lining up the anthropological foundations for method. Then I will offer some psychological techniques to aid one in getting at one's a priori to see how he or she will tend to slant material in order to know when the a priori is seeing and when it has become an organ of distortion.

If science explores the world, religion judges it and determines our attitude towards it. What I shall not employ is the positivistic method of the empirical sciences simply because I find that it is inadequate for a proper understanding of religion. Science, perforce, must take a partial view of flowers, rocks, even people and truth itself. In a word, it is too humble a view of men and things. Religion's graced hubris endows it with a privileged view of the cosmos and places us in it in a way that no partial science -- and they are all that -- can do. Both the historian of religion who is religious and the theologian of religions operate out of this privileged position and it allows them to see the inner life of the subject. Positivistic methods and those employed by non-religious historians and theologians limit one to the outside of things, to the phenomenon. In philosophy it gets one going around in circles about the meaning of meaning without coming up with anything meaningful about anything. This may seem harsh, but try it, as my generation has, and see what judgments that method has made on the world. It can't judge, it can only name without assigning a really significant (telling) schema to the name. And who is to say that the name is correct and not something arbitrary, a sign as we shall call it later? You might rightly say that the religious phenomenon (the outer manifestation of it) is critical to religion. But it is not essential; its inner life is. But, the inner life can only be known when it is communicated, when it becomes a mask. In this sense, then, our masks are our truth, and truth must be our mask. More on this when we come to the section on sign and symbol.

If "Mythology is the shadow cast by language over thought," one must have more than the empirical and linguistic view of *mythos* and *logos*, or the religious figure, in order to see and know him as he is in himself. (3) When Leo Baeck said that the history of religions is the history of language he didn't go far enough. (4) It is the history of people. Man and woman are more than their language, as the whole is greater than the sum of its parts. Mircea Eliade said that the scale creates the phenomenon. (5) To say that one knows the religion or the man when one has made a study of word, doctrine or rite is insufficient. One must step back and see a religious person on a religious scale. Macroscopy informs microscopy as soul does body.

A slight digression is necessary to fill in what I think about language as part of the method. We are is greater than our language and religious people are the scale of our study. In a large sense in creating the word, language creates us. Coming up out of our a prioris word becomes our mask (symbol of our truth) and then, seen for the first time, it is appropriated sending it back into the a priori, the locus of the transcendent, enriching it as it changes it. We grow through our masks, but we must be wary of words which do not symbol the real within us or those whom we study. To see the arbitrary (sign) and mistake it for the necessary or essential (symbol) is to make the word impoverish the reality it means to symbolize and enrich. Any word, no matter how accurate, which stops at the *logos* level, which is the facticity of things devoid of schema and therefore shorn of meaning, impoverishes the thing or person it means to communicate to others. The religious word must go deeper to the *mythos* level in order to endow the *logos* with the deeper and essential meaning of people and things, which is always a religious meaning in the sense that it is transcendent. Any word which communicates only facticity is peripheral to the real meaning of the person or thing. The sticky thing about *mythos* is that it is filled with a richness and resounds with resonances always endowing facticity (*logos*) with portents which cannot be quantified or placed under human control. And the methodological flaw of empirical modernity is that it seeks to control its facts. But one is not in control of *mythos* but is servant before it. It always exceeds the grasp of facticity (*logos*) asymptotically since the transcendent is always greater than we expect. This is why metaphor and poetry suit the *mythos* reality and not prose, and certainly not mathematics. Art is the home of the myth, not science. And any art which sends us into the mythic level of reality, especially human reality, demands an awe which can only be termed religious, whose next of kin is prayer or contemplation (which is a complete emptiness or *kenosis* in which the subject allows the transcendent to pray to itself in him).

Thus, if language is conceived of as *mythos* rather than logos as creating the reality it symbols -- us, since the highpoint of language is talk about us which is we ourselves -- then I would accept it as the material and formal object of both the history of religions and theology: the material object is person as word and the formal object is word considered as person symbolled. *The* category of both disciplines is, therefore, the person. The sign, the word which is arbitrary, serves us. The symbol which creates us in its utterance -- and the spoken word is really the only word in this sense -- also masks us with our humanity as the fig leaf had to be added to our primal parents when they knew their sexual reality was for mutual commerce, but to be hidden at the same time. Knowledge created the myth at its inception.

Art intensifies reality, and when placed at the service of language, especially religious language, it scotches out the necessary abbreviation of the real that an arbitrary positivism places on it -- and all empirical science is arbitrary (on the sign level) in this sense. Art in the service of religion becomes myth. It is a concretization of the real that mere language or science abstracts for its humble task of facticity. The scientist, in searching out the one general element signifying the reality of his discipline, simplifies the complexity of reality. Art in its fusion of the concrete mask with the intensely individualized spirit is *chiaroscuro* because it intensifies the reality it depicts by manifesting it as mystery, while science can of its nature be only *chiaro*. Art intuits the form of the thing itself. Thus, in religion it is art which goes to the heart of the matter in a way that nothing else can. The celebration of the Catholic Mass is a congeries of sights, sounds shapes, touches and ideas all conspiring to allow deep to speak unto deep. (6) The method I espouse is just such an art.

Hence art as a plastic re-presentation of the religious emotion or intuition is, for want of a better word, holistic, while philosophy and the scientific approach mean to be, and are, partial at best. Art as literature is a better approach, therefore, than just plain prose since it derives from a deeper level of man than a mere doctrinal statement done in philosophical prose. Poetry is a more whole approach to religious literature than is prose since its contours and vectors, the textures of its metaphors, catch hold of the soul more than does clear straightforward prose. Parenthetically, the *logos* personality can hardly stand, let alone understand, the *mythos* person. The artist evokes his own reality as he symbols his vision; and even as he reveals himself in his work -- the *chiaro* -- he must hide it so as to preserve its holy vulnerability -- the *oscuro* side of things, the addition of which makes it mythical.

Thus, art is primarily for the artist just as is any human utterance. Only secondarily is it a communication for others; and the more it fully symbolizes himself the more opaque, the more of a mask, his truth becomes. This is why non-representational art infuriates some of us even as it delights us: we are outsiders to a process of revelation; it isn't ours even though it is given over to our perusal, sometimes even having it in our house as an objet d'art. But no one possesses art, one merely observes it. The artist is forever its possessor since it is his symbol.

All art is subject symbolled, not object communicated. One cannot communicate an object. In this sense is everything subject; its intelligibility [*species intelligibilis*], as Aristotle and Aquinas tell us, is the spiritual capacity in it; its ability to communicate as it masks. The basis for my theory of mask is that there is a dark surd within. It is not evil, just an innocent materiality which is, as such, incommunicable. This is, again, why St. Thomas says that we can never fully know the essence of a fly; its materiality is a surd. This dark surd is both a source of delight and pain since it can only be communicated by metaphor, never by discursive reason. The convolutions of the object which make him a self-reflective person, a subject, also make it impossible to reveal him directly. So both principles, our materiality and our spirituality -- they are not our parts, nor are they to be found separately -- are patient of only tangential, somewhat asymptotic approaches. That is why some spiritual masters in both yoga and Christian ascetical theology call the nub of our person a point: it is approached by a curved line and recedes the closer the line gets.

The artist functions as what the poet Rimbaud called a Seer. His creative intuition places him in another mode of consciousness in which the limits of ordinary perception and cognition are either vastly expanded or entirely gone. At times the artist is given things he depicts but does not understand. The Connecticut artist Sebastian Di Stefano, in one of his non-representationslcanvasses, had painted the Hebrew word *Khrisul* (liquidation) painted in it in Hebrew characters. He hung it in a gallery the curator of which was from Israel. Being told what he had done he admitted to having absolutely no knowledge of Hebrew and no intent to say anything about 'liquidation' in it. But it was there, nonetheless, because he is a Seer. The experience is mystical when it takes one to union with all creation: the heavens, the earth, the sun and the sea are perceived as a unity and one is united with them in the breathless cognition that one is directly experiencing one's own materiality. Creating out of this almost manic expansion experience, which many of us call Nature Mysticism, is one of the most powerful experiences one may have. There, one sees reality as an extension of the self; one is literally writing the self into words or painting it into form. Such reality is larger than normal and carries with it a communicability that is beyond ordinary language and form. This is what I mean by being on the myth level, being a Seer or, as the Hebrews called him a *nabi* (Prophet). It is on this level that art, natural mysticism and religion converge. The intuitive cognitions, or inspirations, are not the product of discursive reasoning for words in a writer or planned forms in a painter. What both produce is myth in the sense that the reality is their individual truth universalized in art. Thus the language of both art and religion is mythological, treating of the larger realities in bold print and figure. Given in culture-specificity they burst the bonds of time and space even as they symbol it with supernal perfection. In symbolling themselves and their time and place they transcend it.

If the first phase is expansion the second is a tremendous focusing of the powers in reaching for the correct words in writing, and the harmonic lines in the plastic arts. The first phase was intuition (cognition) of a felt-known kind where the heart and mind fused in knowing as one does in the sexual embrace the Bible called 'knowing' another person. That phase is an undifferentiated knowing in which the person is one with all. The second phase is the differentiating phase in which one reaches for the symbol which bespeaks individuality yet retains the connotation of universality.

It is in this sense that I propose that method be intuitive and an art; that *cor ad cor loquitur* (heart speaks unto heart). The best hermeneutics, the most cogent history and theologies of religion, are done by those endowed with the ability of the Seer, the from time-to-time dilation of consciousness which we call nature mysticism or creative intuition. Not everybody can do this kind of history or theology. Only those who are within a religion have the kind of experience of which the theology of religions writes. Only those gifted as artists among the religious can be the Seer in the expanded consciousness that allows craft to come to experience and symbol it so that its readers can say, "Yes, that's us!"

II
The Symbol Versus the Sign

Karl Rahner has a theory of transcendental symbol which explains what I mean by symbolling the self. His first principle is that each of us is symbolic by nature, and that we attain our nature by expressing ourselves. (7) His second principle merely reverses the first: we also attain our nature by expressing ourselves in symbol. (8) Since, given enough metaphor or simile, everything would ultimately agree with everything else, one would constantly be dealing with merely derivative things whose connections are extrinsic rather than with the essence. What's worse, one would not be able to discern the difference between the intrinsic and the extrinsic. The reason is that by nature the extrinsic sign is an arbitrary agreement of one being with another, whereas, the symbol and its referent are intrinsically connected. One thing expresses the essence of the other and the 'other' becomes itself in being expressed.

57

Each reality is intact in itself and has its own essence and intelligibility. The symbol does more than 'agree with' something else. It is more than 'similar to' the being it symbolizes. The religious symbol, which is the symbol *par excellence*, has an intrinsic, ontological (entitative), connection with the thing symbolized. It bears a fullness which sign cannot. Symbol is thus freighted with being while sign merely alludes to or points to being. (9)

Rahner defines symbol and symbolism thus: The one reality "renders another present (primarily for itself and only secondarily for others) ... (Thus) symbol ... allows the other to be there." (10) This has importance for the historical study of religions since apprehension of the symbol allows one to "be there"; it causes one to 'remember' (*anamnesis* = Gr.) , to evoke a presence fully, which is the essence of good historical method as well as being the heart of the Christian Eucharistic celebration, especially the Roman Catholic version of it.

For Rahner, this attainment of essence in the symbol means that a symbol is the "self-realization of a being in the other," which constitutes the essence of the human person. (11) By this he means that symbol shares the analogy of being with the being it symbolizes. Hence, a being has many modalities; concept and reality bend, and symbol bends as does the reality it figures. The core being bends out to the 'other' in and through symbolism. The symbol is itself. Hence, for the historian or theologian of religions to grasp the symbol is to grasp the inner being of rite, actor, writer, monument or icon. Symbolized and symbol are congruent. The historian becomes what he studies. Eliade put it well when he said , "To treat such alien soil should change the reader and awaken the confessor." (12) One must see, feel and think with the religious believer; and doing this makes one a bit of a believer in the other religion oneself.

Thus, if in a study, I become one with Buddhism, there is a multiplicity in me. This is not a negative quality. All being is plural in its unity. In the Christian religion, even God is plural in the mystery of his unity. Hindus have far less difficulty with this than do we Christians. So this multiplicity is, rather, a positive quality expressive of one's richness and polyvalence. The same is true for God. (13) The plurality "... constitutes itself, by virtue of its origin from an original unity, as the way to fulfil the unity... in such a way that that which is originated and different is in agreement with its origin and hence has ... the character of expression of 'symbol' with regard to its origin." In other words, the symbol does more than agree with its point of origin; it is one with it.

But how does a being become what it is by expressing itself? Rahner sees it happening in the principle : *In tantum est ens cognoscens et cognitum, in quantum est ens actu.* In other words, it is an actual being in so far as it is a knowing one and a known one. One possesses oneself in knowledge and love; i.e. one constitutes oneself in the plurality of knowledge and love and thereby becomes oneself. The opposite is just as true. When one is present to oneself one real-izes himself. One becomes what one is *ad extra* (to others) by being a presence to other humans. In the Christian mold, in a sense, God becomes Himself *ad extra*, in relation to us, by being a presence to us. We share in the same principle and become ourselves in the same way . I am myself when I express myself; the content of my being is knowledge and love. The expression is not disparate or discrete but constitutive. It is a real symbol.

Thus, symbol is the fruition of our being. We become what we are by expressing our being. We express what we feel we are. When that expression is accurate, it is symbol. When it is not, it is sign. So our word becomes an extension of ourselves -- an incarnation of us in symbol form. A symbol which is not arbitrary, but an essential intentional presence of our multi-faceted, rich, personhood. When a man, for instance, vows marriage he becomes marriage, a union of hearts and minds. In knowledge , the knowledge of how he sees himself *qua tale* (as such) he extends himself so that he may be seen and loved by himself. Thus, symbol is primarily for the one doing the symbolizing. If another grasps the symbol by being able to name it correctly, he has hold of one's essence -- partially -- depending on how near to the core of the essence the symbol is.

These pluralities realize the person as the pluralities in God realize him in Trinity. His plurality is essential to him -- and indeed it is His essence. The same is true for us. Our plurality , our symbols, realize us in our being. They are ourselves in act. As God is primarily symbolic in realizing himself "by constituting a plurality" so are we primarily symbolic for the same reason. A being gives itself to the other in symbol and thereby knows and loves itself; it finds itself in the symbol known and loved.

So it is with us. We make a symbol because we know and love the person in the symbol; for the whole person is in the symbol, and , in a sense, becomes the symbol. Thus, the person becomes himself in positing the symbol. (16) He gives himself away in the symbol and by the same act finds himself. He possesses himself and gives himself away in self-expression. This *kenosis* (emptying = Gr.) allows him to 'find' the self. He constitutes himself in this invention and donation.

For instance, suppose we were to be studying Nagarjuna, the cofounder of the Middle Way sect of Mahayana Buddhism early in the Christian era. The donation which we would pursue would be the religious symbolism and religious life of Nagarjuna. His writings are symbols of himself. But to understand the self of Nagarjuna one must see him in his context. He is a Buddhist writing in the flow of Indian religion in general and Mahayana Buddhism in particular. I approach him as a Roman Catholic thinker. My religion, my philosophy and theology are Roman Catholic. I intend to face another religious man (I presume that I am religious for the sake of argument) in a tradition very different from mine. If I wipe away my philosophy and its use in my theology, which is merely a structured attempt at articulating my own religious experience, I leave myself with a person other than myself. This is not only suicidal intellectually, I feel it is impossible. One must be fair and sensitive to the other. How can one do that by becoming something other than oneself? The facticity of the other's a priori, his interiority symbolled in the masks of religious texts or artifacts, is always powerful enough to challenge one's own lacunae and dark spots. So much so, that one's very paradigm might have to change to accommodate the new data. Paradigm shifts are not easily come by, but when they happen one becomes capable of drawing meaning from the anomalous phenomena that one's own paradigm is making a mess of. The power of communicating with another is that it changes one when it is really done on the deepest level. Understanding means change, growth.

Here I would reverse Rahner's first principle (the self-realization of person is in symbol) and say that the symbol is the self-realization of a being in the other, which is constitutive of its essence. (17) A being can be known because it is symbolic in its essence and symbolic for itself. It attains itself as it makes itself known as 'other.' (18) Without this, symbolic being could not be known. This is symbol in its transcendental, original, sense. In this sense, Nagarjuna's work is both a transcendental symbol and a revelation of himself. Essence appears, secondarily, for others to see, but primarily for the person himself to see and love. To reconstruct Nagarjuna's symbol is to raise him to life in the sense that one realizes him; one 'remembers' him.

This is history as *anamnesis*. Nagarjuna did it in evoking the Buddha's teaching in what we know today as the Madhyamika (Middle Way) school of Mahayana Buddhism. He was at once hermeneut and

60

historian in reconstituting the primal religion, its intuitions and values. He discerned the intuition of the Buddha in his hermeneutical work and recreated it in all its uniqueness in himself, thus providing his constituency with the original basis of Buddhism and broadening it organically so that Mahayana could expand as a living extension of that original intuition. In this sense Nagarjuna took the Buddha's advice, and applied it to his own situation; this would be skill in means (*upaya* = Skt.), which is essential in the growth process of the Madhyamika and Mahayana. It was the tool both of renewal and expansion.

This *anamnesis* is critical to both the historian and theologian since theological retrieval is an historical function. In remembering the phenomenon one recalls it to mind and heart, making it present to oneself. The physical scientist measures, by means direct or indirect, and quantifies the results. (19) The historian remembers first of all. Thus, it is a cognitive (intuitive) process. The historian lives in a physical world but deals with symbolic objects in his research. His job is to understand old symbols in the same way in which the originator understood them. The document, monument and rite are the immediate objects of his energies. These symbols are to be examined and will, one hopes, become charged with meaning. They should have the same elan for the historian-hermeneut as they did for the one who wrote them or created them. (20)

The difference between history and science is not in the logic, but in the object. The historian reconstructs the empirical world and adds a symbolic reconstruction. Cassirer feels he is more linguist than scientist. I would state it that he is more historian than scientist, and most of all a Seer-artist since he not only re-presents, but gives impressions which evoke the *Zeitgeist* of the past. He resonates with the time studied through the medium of symbol. Cassirer called him a *ruckwarts gekehrten Propheten* (a retrospective prophet). (21)

In this light, one hopes to reconstruct and then interpret Nagarjuna's experience. Thus the historian must engage in hermeneutics to find the artistic intuition by which he will then ply his learned craft. History collects the *disjecta membra* (strewn limbs) of a culture and fuses them together into a shape and significance which resurrects the original. This is the bits and pieces phase of the method. Where Cassirer called it Palingenesis I prefer anamnesis since it connotes that, more than a mere dry recalling of the past to one's memory, it evokes as it provokes the reality in our imagination and affections. This is why art and history as art converge and become one. They end up on the image and affective level for the practitioner, the reader and the viewer, if the artist is proficient.

It was in this sense that Nagarjuna was an historian. He did what Leibniz spoke of: *On recede pour mieux sauter*, drew back in order to leap higher.

And it is in this sense that our study should coincide with, for instance, Nagarjuna's method and goal. We hope to go back and recreate his inner life and leap above him to see what it means. After the process of anamnesis the historian must always step back from the bits and pieces and say, "*Quid significat?*" ; what does it all mean? The hermeneutical process puts the bits and pieces together only because these shards have evoked something which becomes in him the creative artistic intuition. He means to get at the symbol, discerning that this is symbol and that is sign; this is essential since it is the necessary heart and that is important and interesting, but it is merely the arbitrary extrinsic side of the religion. Cassirer said , "All factual truth implies theoretical truth." (22) Facts are not givens; they are relational. The subject has his own modes of seeing and judging. He employs these to judge the facts. One should begin first with the self -- the seer and judger -- and then procede to the other. One's own a prioris are the very possibility of knowing anything else, of going out to the other to perceive and understand him. It is only in articulating these a prioris, symbolling them, thus allowing them to become our truth masks that we can know others. But, oddly enough, it is only in going out to the other that our own masks appear. Only in relation to the other person , here as other religious person, can we know ourselves. Thus all knowledge is self knowledge. We can only know our prejudices (a prioris, masks) by knowing others. To say that one goes out to another objectively in the sense that one does so without prejudices is a meaningless and , sometimes, mischievous phrase. We may not admit to our prejudices, but they are the sovereigns of our intellect, shaping it and allowing it to see; allowing it to do what constitutes the transcendent capacity of our intellect and heart: to ask a question. Through the aggressivity of question-making we go beyond our present state. This is transcendence, even if no answer comes of it.

Susan K. Langer said that a question is an ambiguous proposition of which the answer is its determination. The question determines the treatment of the subject. (23) Karl Marx felt that the question determines the answer. This could only be so if the a prioris not only endow one with the possibility of knowing, being transcendent, but impose the shape and texture of that knowledge by dint of one's tradition and the rest of one's culture specificity. So, that which allows us to be transcendent, our a priori, also places a limit on the transcendent. In this sense, even God is limited by our limits. Revelation will only bring out the discontinuities evocative of new religions through the continuities we call tradition. Thus, I agree with Langer when she says, "The principles of analysis are really the particular assumptions of an age, a school of philosophy ... and are so obvious that one : i) is unaware of them, and ii) of the limits they impose." (24) One's hidden mask is not just the odd a priori, but a congeries of them which we call a paradigm. Only in the challenge of cognition, going out to the other, does our own makeup emerge. This is why I have jettisoned the phenomenologist's tool epoche if it means that one can do theology or religious studies without presuppositions. Such a flawed method wishes to scotch out one's a priori as prejudice. In doing so one guts oneself of one's paradigms and the possibility of being transcendent in questioning and answering those questions.

III
The Method Applied

We do not have bodies; in a very real philosophical and existential sense, we are bodies. The body is the actuality of the soul. In an Aristotelian and Thomist sense, therefore, we are not composed of body and soul, but soul and prime matter. Hence body is soul (person) actuated. Since this is so, body is the perfect expression and actuality of the soul. In Rahner's language, body is the 'other' which is "produced by soul itself, and hence its expression and symbol..." Therefore it is axiomatic that body is the symbol of the soul since it is its self-realization, and that soul presents itself in and through the body, from which it is distinct. In an analogical sense, to reconstruct Nagarjuna's , or, in a Christian context, Jesus'body from the bits and pieces is to find his soul, his symbol.

The second axiom flowing from Rahner's thought is that, since symbol and symbolized are a unity -- soul and body as one -- "the individual parts of the body are more than mere pieces put together quantitatively to form the whole body; they are... parts... that comprise in themselves the whole..." (25) Symbols work the same in religion as in men and women.

It flows from this that each symbolic religious manifestation, the part which is revealed, contains the whole of the religion in a very real way. There is a person in each organ, in each thought process and volitional act just as there is a whole religion in each celebration of Mass

63

and each mantra spoken. Hence a religious expression can be termed the whole person. A monk is poor, chaste and obedient. His actions are himself . In the same sense is *nirvana samsara*. Chapter XXV of the Mulamadhyamakakarikasof Nagarjuna says in verses 19 and 20 : "There is nothing whatever which differentiates the existence-in-flux (samsara) from nirvana; / And there is nothing whatever which differentiates nirvana from existence-in-flux./ The extreme limit (koti) of nirvana is also the extreme limit of existence-in-flux;/ There is not the slightest bit of difference between these two." (26) The thrust of Nagarjuna's thought is to do away with all false distinctions and even all distinctions, if that were possible. And this is to safgeuard , in its bald simplicity, the religious experience which he sees as the advice given by the Buddha and covered over by so much historical surface noise that it can be neither heard nor followed.

Nagarjuna reveals himself in this text. I am quoting it to exemplify my methodology. I believe that the method outlined in this chapter allows me to see this better than one which would bracket out (epoche) my feelings and philosophical paradigm. Mine is an unabashadly Roman Catholic theology and philosophy, but it certainly seems to coincide with Nagarjuna's in this matter. Further, I am a member of a religious tradition that values contemplation and contemplatives, whose daily joy and chore it is to practice contemplation in order to find God in *all* things. Nagarjuna was also a member of a religion with a living contemplative tradition. When we Catholics use meditation to approach God and see others doing the same to procure their religious ends -- different, but similar -- it gives us some great common ground to occupy. But supposing, in the name of objectivity, I disallowed this central part of my life, scotching it out, and then tried to approach Nagarjuna; What would I see? He would appear topheavy with dialectic, looking for all his philosophy like a proleptic oriental Kant. Suppose, further, that we mistook his dialectic for all there was to Nagarjuna. We might be tempted to call his religion a philosophy instead of a dialectics flowing out of and subservient to religious experience. If we did that we would see only half of all there is to see in him. If, in the name of objectivity and ecumenism, we followed the lead of some of our western brothers who see little value in contemplation , which is their privilege, and predicated the same tags of Nagarjuna as they do, we should be untrue to ourselves and to the religious person studied. I 'see' more of Nagarjuna when I do not bracket my own religious doctrine, feelings and philosophy. If I find that they get in the way of seeing, and I will know soon enough when my colleagues apprise me of my blindness-due-to-Catholicity,then I can work through them. When one is aware of one's prejudices one can do quite handy things with and through them. Since they happen to be part of one's makeup and world-outlook, it is very difficult,-- no impossible! -- to divest oneself of them. So, for all the reasons given above, one should use them as an organ of perception and cognition. It is not a cognitively bad thing to be Roman Catholic; that faith gives me my set of assumptions, shaping my cognitive faculty so it can know. And when it doesn't do the job for me, what then?

Can we learn new paradigms? Certainly! That's what formation processes are. That's what happens in schools, that's what happens in novitiates, in military training, at our father's or mother's knee, in -- God help us!-- that most imperious novice master of them all, graduate school and a doctoral program. We are 'domesticated' by our mentors, the partial progenitors of our a prioris. The rest of the a priori is there by birth, by genetic -- racial -- code or learned through formative experiences. We learn them and we can change them, though only with great courage. Ernest Becker in his *The Denial of Death* finds the roots of mental illness in the failure of courage, which failure is an impotency before phenomena which demand that we change to meet demands beyond our formation processes. The psychological concept of cathexis means that what we've invested ourselves heavily in can be changed only with great difficulty since that area of our mind is heavily charged with psychic energy. It takes guts and faith in the goodness of being, as well as in God's goodness, to grow -- which is to be certain in knowledge, and unsure of feeling.

This means that our a prioris are organs both of cognition and anti-cognition; the blind spots we pick up from family or along the way. This is why Kuhn's hypothesis on paradigms provoked such a hue and cry in the scientific community: they don't just 'know' their assumptions, they 'believe' them without testing them. If they tested and challenged them all of us who have followed that path know that our Ph.D's would have been in jeopardy. Every a priori is, therefore, a double bind.

This brings us to prejudice as a cultural force. All this includes religion, home and school, language, and race. In a word, all that goes into making up the warp and woof on one's human life: politics, God, parents, etc. These are aprioristic, since they hit us on such a deep level that we are unaware that we have a culture. We think that this is the way things must be since this is the way they are. Vital truths become vital lies when it is necessary to preserve the inner peace of an individual or the cohesiveness and identity of a society, whether that society be

65

church or the academy. Blind spots are not only there, they are to be expected. Epoche fled them since it fears our inner -- sectarian or ethnic -- darknesses. With Paul Ricoeur I say that it is only by knowing these darknesses that we can know our goodness, what Rahner called our original affirmation -- the fact that, at our core, we are good. The closer we get to that core the more feral our fragility becomes. What began as only a sinless weakness, a wound to be healed, becomes a ravening, sinful beast. The root of method, therefore, is a faith in our own humanity. This faith antecedes religious faith logically, and is perhaps all many have attained today. Yet it is salvific, if St. Paul to the Romans is to be believed. And why not believe him? Thus, Enlightenment 'objectivity' rides on a timorousness and agnosticism which fears to go inside because a beast or an Irish pastor might be there. It fled both to become, what? More truthful? If God has to come in by the side door of our universities, then they can only be 'partiversities', fragmented things which fear the great questions because the pope or the Moral Majority might be coming in with them.

Moreover, I think that we are somewhat encoded, by gene or ethhic group or by continent or by religion or by the whole 'schmiere' that we call culture, to act in a certain way. David C. McLelland has done work on national consciousness (*The Roots of Consciousness*, Van Nostrand), and as I said above, cognitive psychologists like Daniel Goleman have demonstrated my thesis very well. I think that we are routed to go one way or another by our roots to clan, culture and religion; not totally so, since we are free, but we are front-loaded to go one way or another before we even know what's happening to us. This is why I think the transcendent is radically different for the differing religions. India was made for Hinduism and Buddhism, just as desert people were made for *Ur* Judaism and Islam. My thesis slips more into the realm of hypothesis when we see the diffusion of Christianity, Buddhism and Islam across cultural lines. But then, didn't Buddhism's device of 'skill in means' (*upaya*=Skt.) make it capable of moving from a non-theistic religion to a theistic one, from a religion without bell, book and candle to one with all that in profusion? And didn't Sufism perform the same function for Islam in former times and isn't it performing it today? Ayatollahs don't win converts, Sufis do. What I am saying is that there is not one transcendent on the esoteric level, as so many theologians and religionists say. There are many.

It comes to this: the a priori is an inchoative faith, in the sense that faith is an organ of vision and a radical openness to the goodness, intelligibility and loveableness of things. Hence, we see because we

66

believe, not vice versa. Prejudice allows vision. Believing in this sense is a set of assumptions about the goodness of people and things and that these assumptions recompose reality, but according to the dictates of that particular religion. Thus, what each faith imagines to be real is so for that religion. Modernity is a paradigm which has up until recently pooh poohed this notion. But latter day criticism of science in the form which Kuhn et al. are offering show that models are the geometry of the mind as much as of extramental reality. *Ur* Buddhism and Zen get one to one's unique Buddhanature with immediacy and definitiveness, but it is an a priori comfortable with the fact that the peace of nirvana exists in the blind spots of samsara: the religion courts the sadnesses of endless repetitive lives in order to find peace and end the vital redundancy of karma.

This brings me to a very important point. Each faith is an a priori and each a paradigm-become-mask. And along with those aspects of our feeling-knowing capacity goes a sensibility. I hold that Protestant spirituality -- and all systematic theology is an articulation of the group's religious experience plus the meta-experience of the Book -- has its strengths and weaknesses when brought to other religions. Catholics have their strengths and weaknesses as well. Groups say what part of their shared experience can be put into words and which words it can be put into. Say 'transubstantiation'in an old-fashioned Protestant seminary, and the pictures fall off the wall. Say 'Luther' or 'Faith without works' to an old-line Catholic and you have a fight on your hands. [Does this mean that the social construction of reality shapes which experience God can give? I think so. Protestants are as good as Catholics but have no saints or miracles in their spiritual lexicon. In fact, until most recently, they haven't even liked the word 'spirituality'. It smacks of monks and other-worldly asceticisms long since jettisoned. Does this mean that Protestants interdict the very possibility of having saints or wonders due to a prohibitory schema or paradigm? Possibly. The ramifications of this from a Christian point of view are chilling ecumenically and missiologically. It seems to mean that there can be no mass conversions since Group Think forecloses the possibility. But prevenient grace is the category God has worked with when it comes to salvation. Just a thought.]

The underlying assumption of method in religious studies and the theology of religions is "Don't get personal." But everything is personal. That's my point.

I offered an example of a Protestant blind spot and a Roman Catholic locus of vision -- mysticism: we Catholics have been beating our breasts long enough, it's time to say what we have going for us, too. Protestant spirituality long ago eschewed mysticism as an ideal. It is based on the rejection of the *analogia entis* (analogy of being), a concept of grace which makes the Catholic ideal a mystical one. The classical Protestant idea of grace has been one of extrinsicism where God does not get involved with our interiority in the same way as he does in Catholicism; this is based on Luther's reading of Romans where grace is so potent that it is otiose to go within, staying outside is enough because, like the Centurion, we are not worthy that he enter the house, so say but the word. So, as Luther said, *pecca fortiter* (if you are in a situation where sin is a necessity, sin bravely). The Protestant sensibility is a secular spirituality, one attuned to finding God in one's workaday relations. The Catholic sensibility is one more attuned to the mystical, where God acts on one's affectivity as a felt-known. [One of the reasons the modern-industrial-technological world passed Catholicism by was that it was consciously holding on to a non-secular paradigm and sensibility. It was at one remove from Protestantism and the direction of modernity and post-modernity, which direction is secular, not sacred.]

Saying all this leads me to conclude that it is easier for a Catholic to 'do' Buddhism or Hinduism than it is for a Protestant because Catholicism is a mystical religion. Frederick Streng's brilliant essay on Nagarjuna's idea of Nothingness concludes that Nagarjuna's religion was a philosophy, not a mysticism. Anyone who has lived in a Catholic milieu as I have, anyone who has employed meditation as prayer and practiced a form of spirituality which opens one to the mystical, knows almost immediately upon reading Nagarjuna that his dialectics are a secular mind-blower to keep the unwashed away from his holy, which is a religious experience, a mysticism, though not the same type of mysticism as their experience. Read Streng and do a phenomenology of the book. What you come up with is a secularized Protestant or a secularized person making Nagarjuna into one. This is exegesis, not exegesis. Streng read his a priori into Nagarjuna, even though at the beginning of the book he said that he was methodologically without presuppositions. There is a blind spot there, one that needs to be exposed. Hence, a Catholic sensibility should render one subject t to it more apt to come up with acceptable results than one without it.

I am maintaining that mysticism is a blind spot for classical Protestants. Karl Barth deplored it, and both Luther and Calvin rejected not only its enthusiasms, but the concept of grace that underlay it:

namely, one in which there is an entitative change in the person receiving God's grace. This was, after all, the major theological battle fought between Roman Catholicism and Evangelical Protestantism. All this leads me to say that I advocate operating out of one's a priori, but it must be constantly challenged by the facticity of the subject in the other religion or in one's own religion. The power of criticism and a docility in the true sense of that word -- a willingness to learn, to change, to be corrected no matter the pain -- will help to show up the blind spots. Maybe we can't ever see some points. But, at least, knowing this through the criticism or the uncomfortable pushiness of another's reality making our certitudes uncertain, we can realize our blindness, and operate accordingly. But, whatever our ocular acuity, we see or don't see because of our a priori. It operates us, we don't operate it. It does so since it is the heart and center of the transcendent. We serve it. But as it gets closer to our ethnic center, culture or religion, to our own facticity, then we begin to manipulate it as individuals and groups. What gives the ring of truth to our studies is if they tingle with the sounds of necessity, if they don't sound arbitrary. When we have something necessary for the faith of the self, then we have the symbol of that faith or our own symbol: we have its mask, and that mask, our mask, is its and our truth. The higher human powers are hidden and known only by inferences drawn from their visible effects, from their symbols or *logos* masks; or from images and metaphors, the non-discursive symbols which are their *mythos* masks. For us Christians, Christ is the ultimate mask, a chiaroscuro sacrament of God in which the Holy appears hidden in the secular. The a priori of God appears in family ritual since it is behavior which manifests not only our lacunae, but also our Pleroma (the fullness of God in the Holy Spirit).

Endnotes for Chapter III
Truth is Our Mask: The A Priori Revealed

1. Leo Baeck, *The Essence of Judaism*. New York: Schocken Books, 1967, p. 129.
2. Ibid., p. 129.
3. Ibid., p. 92.
4. Ibid., p. 91.
5. Mircea Eliade, *The Quest*. Chicago, 1969, p. 7.
6. Ernst Cassirer, *An Essay on Man*. New Haven: Yale, 1970, p. 143.
7. Karl Rahner, *Theological Investigations, vol. IV, More Recent Writings*, London: Darton, Longman and Todd, 1974, p. 224.
8. Ibid., p. 234.
9. Ibid., p. 225.
10. Ibid.
11. Ibid., p. 234.
12. Eliade, op. cit., pp. 61f.
13. Rahner, op. cit., p. 225.
14. Ibid., p. 229.
15. Ibid.
16. Ibid., pp. 229f.
17. Ibid., pp. 234.
18. Ibid., p. 231.
19. Cassirer, op. cit., p. 174.
20. Ibid., p. 175.
21. Ibid., pp. 177f.
22. Ibid., p. 174.
23. Susan K. Langer, *Philosophy in a New Key*. Mentor Paperback, p. 16.
24. Ibid., p. 16.
25. Rahner, op. cit., p. 247.
26. Nagarjuna, *Mulamadhyamikakarikasof Middle Way*. Trans. by Frederick Streng and found in his *Emptiness, a Study in Religious Meaning*. New York, Abindgon, 1967, p. 217.
27. Ernest Becker, *The Denial of Death*. London: The Free Press, 1973.

CHAPTER IV

Method:

The First Moment:
The Secular A Priori

In this essay on method I have faulted Frederick Streng for not seeing the experience of Emptiness [Shunyata, Skt.] as the Buddhists see it: that is, as an experience, a spirituality, what we would call a mysticism, not a philosophy. As such, I cited Streng for a cardinal failure due to his and his forebears' desensitization to the mystical element in religion; that his and their strength is in their fusion of secularity with Christian spirituality. But there is more to it than that since there must be a weakness there if he and so many trained like him fail to 'see' what is there in another religion. He and other Protestant scholars in the history and theology of religions would do well to absorb some Roman Catholic spirituality, which is a mystical spirituality, since we seem to have an easier time with the other mystical religions than he and they do. This is a challenge; I know that. Their thought has been a challenge to us Roman Catholics for four centuries. We Catholics have finally had sense enough to allow Protestant thought into our hearts and minds (our felt-known) in order to 'see' it. We have been challenged by it and changed for the better by it. Vatican II and the massive reformation it keyed are evidence of our sincerity. We have sat at the feet of Protestant mentors, in their universities, been taught by them, doctored under them. Both the classic Catholic thinkers and the best Protestant scholars are sources for shaping our faith, our a priori. Now it is time to repay our great debt to those masters from the other Christian communions. Precisely how I would improve Mr. Streng's vision, which is the dominant one in North American religious studies, is through changing his a priori; and this can come largely through a methodological revision on his part.

Before I offer my final views on method it becomes necessary to show how Protestant secularity has, I think, improved our Roman Catholic vision; changed our a priori and its active moment, our paradigm so that we can see both our own culture and our religion better. After doing that, I shall outline how the contemporary Protestant vision falters as a theology, possibly due to its concept of Jesus and the Church: that it is a softer and diffused vision and theology of the Incarnation and the

71

Church over against a Catholic one which is 'firmer' on Jesus' human divine presence left us in Church and Sacrament.

Much of what I have to say deals with masks and their necessity when they symbol our truth, and the necessity to unmask -- violently, if necessary -- if our masks are inauthentic, depicting at best the arbitrary (signs) instead of our essences (symbols). I will speak of the necessary moment of remasking after we have passed through the fiery moment of criticism, the moment of unmasking. And then I shall give a recapitulation of my method as thus far given in this essay and finish it by an in- depth explication and systematics of what I consider my method.

In any method the person is central: the person of the scholar, the person of God or Buddha, and the person adhering to one's own or another's religion. One begins, then, and ends with person in all religions and any methodology purporting to treat of them. Getting 'at' the person must be first on the agenda; the person as subject and the other subject person whom we unfortunately call 'object'; 'other' would be better. The first moment of method is to get at oneself; the manifestation of one's mask is first; then one puts together the bits and pieces of one's hidden but sovereign paradigm; that done, one is opened up to the passive side of paradigm, which is an a priori (*prejudicium*, or in the vernacular of the German transcendentalists,a *Vorbegriffe*). When one reaches that level one is at home in the transcendent Self, which is also home to one's God. But getting there is no easy task intellectually or emotionally. One must go 'at' one's a prioristic core with courage, honesty and a delicacy begotten of healthy self love. To press one's suite tends to drive the transcendent away; it evanesces quite easily.

The Secular A Priori

First off, one must rip away the mask of inauthenticity. Marx, Freud and Nietzsche serve nicely as models for this. They challenged the God of their day in order to denude his image in us. Seeing how they operate serves two purposes: First, it gets rid of false gods. There is nothing better than a healthy iconoclasm in the religious life. Yahweh himself is the supreme model of this. Genesis is a book filled with healthy atheism, painfully ridding God's people of divine surrogates by smashing their images, leaving only an empty tabernacle full of God and surrounded by a scree of once divine lieutenants. Second, when the false gods are gone man and woman can know themselves as they are: as images of God. The nineteenth-century critics of religion knew that there was no way they could talk to religious people about this and be understood. When one speaks of God one overpowers one's auditor with the *impedimenta* of over thirty centuries of God. One doesn't see much of God there, and much less -- sometimes almost nothing -- of us. To find the self, then, in our day it is necessary to pass through the death dealt by criticism. God must withdraw so that we may find what's left: ourselves in what we call our secularity.

The first step of method, therefore, speaks of our worldliness, not our creatureliness; the latter can come only much later. What appears first is us, not God or our creaturely link with him. Just us, no more and no less. But that is a tall order. And it has been filled in our day. Not that we have developed a complete anthropology; we can't unless it be done in the light of faith. But faith, first of all, waits to compose reality while we go about discovering the worldly reality. It means that we must 'see' the world and our worldly selves for the first time. From our mother's knee, our religious a priori has not allowed us to see our neighbor *qua tale*, but only as children of God because that a priori so shapes our vision that we can see no other.

The first movement of the cognitive and loving faculty is a faith in this secularity revealing itself in us; a faith in it for itself. Later, it will become a religious faith because what we see is God's creature. That faith in secularity fuses with a faith in the self and things as God's creations, and this composes our identities, our masks. William F. Lynch, S.J. says that such faith composes our eyes, our minds and hearts. (1) All men and women have a faith in secularity, some have one in God because things and people are good and worth the vulnerability which religious faith imposes. Both secular and religious faith are an openness to the self allowing us to go out to others. Some faiths are more open than others, enabling one to see more of the other, and therefore to go to him more easily and fully.

If it is difficult to see the secular we must clear away both the detritus and even the constructive aspect of faith in order to find the self and its world. Faith is so culture-specific that even at its best it can 'blind' one to the inner and outer secular reality. The first principle in seeing the secular is this: The secular is *unconditional* and *autonomous*. These are the secular polarities Lynch discerns and they seem to work for our task.

Unconditionality refers to the rediscovery that we do not stand as a symbol for anyone or anything. We are men and women, persons in our own right, not standing for the Church, the state or for any thing or 'ism'. We are individuals standing for nothing more ultimate than ourselves. This means that one doesn't have to go to another to find one's truth; in this sense, even to God. If we are his images, and he can think, so can we. If he is an individual, responsible to himself, so are we. If he is free, so are we. (Of course all this is the language of analogy.) In this sense, religion accepts the truth of humanity in order to be truthful to itself. We find our moral and intellectual truths within. That places an enormous burden on us to be truthful with ourselves. It leaves us naked with our truth and truths. In the truth and its nakedness we discover conscience, the adult's ability to go it alone into the truth of the situation and live with the *chiaroscuro* of it, and with the consequences of following that naked intellection. This is the meaning of our autonomy. It is to be found in our unconditionality, but it is not intellectually anterior to it. Both are the roots of our humanness and humaneness.

Another meaning of unconditioned is that life is an absolute, an ultimate and does not seek a legitimization outside itself. (2) In this sense, we are not imitations of any transcendent. We are a transcendence ourselves; our truth and transcendence are within. Nothing, not religion or God, shapes us in such a way that we cannot stand on our own without it. This is what Marx and Freud and the atheistic humanists of the age are trying to tell us. Autonomy leaves us naked before our own human ultimacy. Our loves bear responsibilities that only the honest and strong can bear. In cheap religion the masks of inauthenticity, rooted in a false perception, which is unripe or immature, become a morality which sees God's will as coming from the outside. But the truth is that God's will, what we call morality, derives from the inside, from the autonomous conscience. When morality in an individual or a religious collectivity derives from the outside it becomes just that, derivative and vapid; just what Freud knew it was and railed against in his lifelong critique of religion and the moral immaturity he found in it. If God's will comes from within our intellect and will then the root of it is a secular felt-known, a human a priori which allows us to go beyond the situation to discern the good and the wicked and all that entails. Hence, to find the religious existential, go within the secular -- human -- transcendental existential. The Kingdom of God is within you because you are within you. We create the right thing, the moral, by the unconditionality of our wishing; and this unconditioned -- untrammeled -- cognitive sense flows out into the autonomy of our nature.

Neither reason nor religious meaning foreclose our potential and truth. Nothing shapes us in such a way that we cannot stand on our own without it, not even God; the good atheist abounds in our secular culture.

Men and women wear masks of inauthenticity-- of conditionality and heteronomy -- because they mistakenly seek their identity in them. Such masks as muted secularity -- when the individual cannot abide the pain of seeking one's full truth in a conscience grown up and still growing -- are perversions of the human. In such an individual and the shallow culture he spawns, there is the cult of the expedient rather than of the good and true and the unifying and integrating force that this troika of transcendentals has been from time immemorial. It is a fervor for the shallow and inhuman that causes us the pain of our secular immorality. Unconditionality allows us to grow past the constrictions and aberrant a prioris of our youth -- and all cultures and religions misstate truth to some degree or other and so twist the transcendental a priori -- to find the symbol beyond our intellectual, moral and emotional formation; to find the word or artistic metaphor or form to depict our truths. But the thing about the unconditionality of the secular human is that it is not infinite. To find the self opens one up to the limits of that self. One may, in time must, think the unthinkable, but not the inhuman or inhumane unthinkable. Growth comes only when we think what hasn't been thought or couldn't or shouldn't be thought; but evil comes when we forget that we are limited in the very wellspring of our humanity. We are infinities limited by the surds of our condition: willed or unwilled evil, disease both physical and mental, and death. These limits constantly throw us back onto the truth that while we can and must revel in the luxury of our unconditionality and autonomy, we find that we cannot know all that we want and need; that we cannot love all whom we want and need and should love; and we cannot do everything that we can conceive of. In the fonts of our invention of the human we find our transcendence, but know by experience that we do not shape it, but that it shapes us; that we do not choose it but that it chooses us even if we are its finders; that we do not rule it, even if we found it lying unused in the inner recesses of our minds, but, rather, that we are the servants of that which we grow into: we serve transcendence when it becomes the Transcendent. We serve it , but only when we act in the naked autonomy of growth. There is a tension there: service in autonomy. Therefore, religion begins in secular autonomy. This is our human opening to religion and God. But it can never be anterior to the human.

Religious masks are the easiest to falsify. This is why a cheapened religious transcendent causes us to become so inauthentic, to deny the imperatives of our a prioris to grow. We choose the 'cheap grace' Bonhoeffer spoke of when we deny the ability of our minds and hearts to find the good, the true and the one within us and within the human dimension; the samsaras of our lives. Such religion is easy in morality, even if it causes untold pain and damage in our lives, which it frequently does when one's principles become one's prisons; or worse, procrustean beds to lop off not only our own intellectual or emotional or intellectual limbs, but those of others; especially if we hold positions of authority in any religion but have no inner human, secular, unconditionality and autonomy in which true religion can grow. If there is nobody home, then the inauthentic becomes the surd covering the healthy a priori that abides in all of us. If we take our model from the Christ without, then he never comes to make his home with us as he promised he would. How could he? There's nobody home and God is an exuberance, a trinity of persons demanding a response. God is no fool, triply so. He will not spend his presences when they would be the sound of a tree falling in the forest where nobody was there to hear them. Just as sound means nothing unless there is a person or animal to hear it, so personal presence is nothing and nowhere unless there is a person to be present to. This is why God must be trinitarian: he must be present to another person. The teaching of circumincession ensures that God's presence is never otiose, never extended uselessly. In us, too, this presence must be had in one who is home; i.e. grown in all his unconditionality and autonomy. God would not be heteronomous to us since he made us like himself: autonomous. When religion makes heteronomous noises it is a sure sign that it is entering a period of decay when only repression can keep us 'in line'. When autonomy can't do the trick, then the mediocre or faithless resort to repression.

The most difficult task of this first moment, ripping off the masks of our inauthenticity to get at the uncondtioned and autonomous secular is getting past the *simulacra* of those twin poles of our humanity. Our very absoluteness, our Godlikeness, does create a curiosity to go beyond those fictions, however. When we cannot, that becomes anxiety. When we can, it becomes anxiety. The one anxiety kills, the other frees, both hurt. Neurosis is an anxiety rooted in word poverty (3) -- the poverty of a too narrow childhood formation; and it is then that our prejudices cannot be organs of vision, but become, instead, organs of distortion, the mask-makers that destroy the possibility of our gospel dream. Neurosis happens when there is no possibility of action or choice; when we hug stupidly to the possibility range of our childhood. Our identities are joined tentatively out of words, and when growth pushes from within to scramble the mask of words, we tend to hold to them as to our mothers. It is then that what Marie Louise von Franz calls the return to the mother happens. To free oneself of one's destructive masks -- a bondage to a mother complex -- one must allow the darkest, bloodiest feelings and rages to bubble to the surface to allow oneself to 'see' (the beginning of our vision of the church or of anything is our vision of ourselves, since we must love the other as we love **ourselves**) ourselves through the blind touch of feeling. It is this that overcomes the amnesia suffered after Eden when we forgot who we were. This feeling is an *anamnesis* (a remembering who we are) which allows us the revelation -- the vision -- of who we really are. And that will always be a good thing, since where we are is who we are; and where we are is where the self and God are. So when we go to where the heart and mind really are, to our unconditioned wish and thought, to where we generate the good and the true, we really begin to feel our anger, our 'gut's' movements. Things begin to happen like suicidal impulses, a sense of despair, a sense of putrefaction, hungry oral needs -- these desperate cravings and compulsions that return us to our bodies. These needs are what the novice yogin calls his *vasanas*, i.e. that which begins as need or compulsion in both Buddhist or Christian spirituality. The pained and fearful awareness of these needs ultimately becomes , at the end of the process in both Buddhism and Christianity, an immediacy with one's own biology. Then the value of our suffering will precede its meaning. Seeing begins before knowing. We will birth the good and the true before we baptize it. Feeling begins our seeing; and this is a return to our childishness and delivers us to it. This is humiliating because we feel inferior before our feelings. We begin to learn that feeling is 'the art of the small'. (4) This same journey must accompany any opening up to another religion; it is a return to a mother we never knew, but a human mother nonetheless; and she will become our mother in the study if we do it correctly, even should we never become a member of that 'other' religion.

All this may sound like auto-eroticism, and I suppose it really is. It is falling in love with the emergent self, falling in love with one's own love and ideas as truth. The trap is not to worship oneself, to preach *amour-propre* as a secular or religious gospel. The thing is to let love, one's truth seen and appropriated, become one's Truth in both secularity and religion. This means that we must let love shape us, for that is our deepest truth; love and good. And we don't trust that in our own lives; no wonder that we don't trust it in studying other religious people. So we use dogma and virtue, church and sacrament, vision and mission as partial visions, partial faiths and missions to preach that fragmented vision. When this happens we are secular or religious prophets preaching particulate faiths, truncated apostles staying too close to the shore since we fear to put out into the deep of ourselves and of others. We are called to grow, to let our self free in our midst -- for we can contain it with our frightened laws. This call to go within is what Jungian psychologists call returning to our feminine side, to the dark, wet recesses of our minds and hearts to be born again , not through our wall-tight secularities or religions, both born of either hubris or fear -- hubris when we fail to be little or limited, fear when we fail to be large in the experience of our feelings, what we deprecate as less than mind and heart. This is how we rip off the masks of our inauthenticity to get at our real humannness, our secularity. This is what William F. Lynch meant when he said that the root of such secularity is a faith, a radical openness to the goodness within and without recomposing the imagination within (the poesis aspect of the a priori) so that it may recompose reality for us. Such humanistic faith allows the unconditionality and autonomy to seek their own level. The faith of each will be the each of faith; i.e. the openness of the individual is incommunicable since it is the cause of his a priori, his very individuality. And that is unique to each person. That is why the conscience and loves of each of us mustn't be those of our neighbor, lest they become heteronomous and constricting, thereby becoming inauthentic masks twisting the transcendent potential of the a priori into shapes rendering it incapable of knowing or loving either the self or anybody or anything else.

Thus this is the first step of our method: finding our own unconditionality and autonomy as persons so that we may later go out to others. This is a faith anterior to the faith known in religion, but on which each religion must be built.

But, what are the inauthentic masks I as a Catholic scholar have to remove in order to descend to allow truth to emerge as my mask? In the Reformation, Catholics opted for authority in freedom; Protestants for freedom with authority. The emphasis has made it easy for Catholics to resort to authoritarianism when true authority eluded them. Thus, an overweening attitude towards the statements of the hierarchy besets the Catholic scholar. In order to get to one's autonomy and unconditionality a broadly spread, deep, critical mentality must accompany the scholar in reading the words of any official statement. Dogmatic fundamentalism is the besetting sin of Catholicism; the Biblical variety dogs Protestantism on the conservative side and antinomianism on the liberal side. The underlying problem is one of placing dogma together with religious experience. Sixteenth-centuryCatholicism was rife with false mysticism; so much so that the first Jesuits, happily enjoying a dilating immediacy with God, were told to downplay their mysticism since Rome was looking with a gimlet eye at any mystics those days. The Jesuits decreed that henceforth their young men were to be taught meditation and not the joys of contemplation in order that their active apostolate not be suppressed by Rome. Experience became subordinated to authority and its symbolic hierophany in dogmatic statements in the Roman communion, as a result. Protestants placed a primacy on the immediate experience with the Holy Spirit which they found in mulling over the words of the Scriptures. But for both, psychologically and epistemologically, experience antecedes its formulation.

The masks we Catholics must watch for and rip away when found are those of mistaking for faith a cowering attitude before official *pronunciamenti*; we must learn to distinguish between a dogmatic hierophany (and a high-level authoritative statement, especially a papal one is a religious such a religious experience for a Catholic) and its notional truth in order to stay true to both our autonomy and that of God and his religion. To get to an authentic a priori, one which is instinct with the radical openness bespoken by unconditionality and autonomy, one must pass through the fire of learning; learning the history and meaning of dogma in sufficient amounts that one begins the stripping away of false faith, which is credulity. It is a cheap grace that infantilizes the individual and has, at times, the power to paralyze a whole church. With Protestants, the masks cheap grace takes are a misuse of the freedom of the Holy Spirit,of protesting when they should be listening -- a lack of the contemplative sensibility -- the openness of faith allowing them to scc and hcar thc words of thc gospel and its Holy Spirit. Further, with the return of mysticism from the periphery of Roman Catholicism, my task is easier in getting down to the a priori of things, behind and within the mask of truth. The Catholic concept of grace is based on the *analogia entis* where we participate in God inwardly. With the return of true mystical contemplation, especially with the Jesuits' return to the original way of giving the *Exercitia Spiritualia* of St. Ignatius Loyola, one is ushered into one's self and taken up by God in an immediacy which can only be mysticism. It changes one because one is so loved that one opens up to see the self as it really is; for the first time. One is so carefree and open in faith that one doesn't care to hide behind the psychological masks of untruth which we call character or personality. One is radically simplified. But this is to get ahead of our moments. The first moment is to rip away the masks of inauthenticity to get to our secularity where we can alter ourselves through criticism -- the

79

felt-known of the a priori is the product of an affective-cognitive power which can be changed. Criticism in this sense is an epistemological, psychological and ontological (entitative) critique demanding and causing a change in our a priori and thus changing the transcdendent for us. Thus criticism is the first moment; and it alters our masks (symbols) because their cause, our a prioris and paradigms, have been changed.

Such criticism challenges categories like the supernatural, which didn't come into play in Roman thought until St. Thomas Aquinas, and which had been taken over much more by Protestants than Catholics. But, for Catholics, too, it has played a major role in pegging things. It has changed the a priori of faith; so much so that it is sometimes difficult to find the human inside the divinized (Catholic) or graced, faith-filled , saved (Protestant), men and women holding to those creeds. If there is a supernatural then there must be a natural; but it is useless multiplication where the 'human' would serve just as well. God and the supernatural have overwhelmed our ability to see and be human. The movement to secularity is in large part merely one in which we are trying to find ourselves under the weight of centuries of supernatural verbiage. The category supernatural, not what it was trying to symbolize -- which is a divinized existential, a human being beloved of and adopted by God --, has become not just otiose, it is harmful. It so freezes one within oneself that conscience and heart cannot find the self without doing real violence to oneself.

If God is to have commerce with us at all, then it will have to be on our terms, which terms are human. We cannot understand things divine; he keeps telling us that in the Scriptures. Thus the Incarnation is not only his final word, it is his final Word to us that **the** paradigms or grammars of God are men and women. The Second Vatican Council's document on revelation (Dei Verbum) has it that Jesus is the category of revelation, a person, not a theological category. Thus, Jesus is God's declension and his actions are the verbs of God; but they are human nouns and verbs, inflected and conjugated with our rules, not his. Religion and the theologians who serve it have reversed the tables. We didn't want a human being, we wanted Transfigured Jesus, not plain old Jewish Jesus. The Scriptures tell us that the Apostles, especially Peter, looked up to the previously Transfigured Jesus, whom the Father had underwritten as his Son, and saw "Jesus, and him alone." Just him, no more. The upshot is that the arena of God is man and woman. Secularity is not to rid us of transcendence, though it has when wrongly interpreted. It is to allow full scope to our humanity. Religion begins after that. The trouble is that we were baptized long before that; that we are already religious and have to look for the secular self within a religious self. There's the dilemma; either the one or the other? It is a false dilemma and not a real problem at all; though it is a painful process. Process, therefore, not problem. God will take care of the religious side; we must care for the human side of the ledger.

Hence, to find ourselves we must find our secularity. To find God, or be found by him -- which is more accurate if we go by God's definition as beyond our powers to find -- we must find our free-standing autonomous and unconditioned, naked, self. But the naked self must always be covered over with the clothing, not just fig leaf, of symbol. The a priori is the garment of the self; the asymptotic, shy, terribly subtle core of our personality which must be hidden because of its subjectivity. We can never fully objectivize the self since it is subject. We always find ourselves clothed, as were our first parents in the Garden after their educational experience with the tree and the first teacher, Lucifer, whose name means light-bearer. Both secular faith and religious faith clothe the self with categorical garments. Their seams are the networks of our cognitive and affective apparatus, bringing meaning and love out of our experiences; staving off chaos and insanity, fostering the volitions that fulfill our deepest yearnings.

The high point of this first moment is, then, an *anamnesis*. All human knowing and loving is an attempt to 'remember' who we were in the Garden. The symbol 'remember' (*anamnesis*) is an attempt to get at a resolution to the rending human experience that we know we are more than we are; that we are meant for more than we have; that we are better than we know. Becoming human in root secularity means that for the first time we know the nakedness of the knowledge of good and evil. To choose the one or the other demands that we live with its consequences; that we either do what we are meant for, the good, or suffer the loss of self once again. The a priori, once uncovered by the honesty and pain of the search for our humanity, can be lost once again; possibly for good, if our volition is radical enough.

What is the task of *anamnesis*? To imagine the real. If faith is belief in, trust in, the real, then what is the real? If the secular is unconditional then the task of imagination as secular is to seek and find that secular unconditionality as to find itself. Thus, the task of the secular is one of imagination. We must find, conjure up, the real once again. If the imagination is separated from either the intellect or will then false secularities arise such as empiricism and positivism. These latter are the patrimony of modernity which said that such concepts as Truth and

81

Reality are too much to control, too much to ask us to handle. As such, then, the scientific -- empirical -- method is too modest. It validates and can validate only what it knows, never drawing the big picture of men and women, or world. But men and women are not scientists at heart, they are humans. Their task is to draw that large canvas and find reality. Freud, Marx and Nietzsche only began the task when they stripped away false gods and constructs in religion allowing immaturity, injustice and mediocrity to pass as the masks of God and as our human-religious masks. The next step in the process is to find the new synthesis; a step which we have not taken fully, but which seems in process nonetheless.

When imagination fails it invents slogans, tales, inaccurate categories and inadequate dogmas -- depending on whether the arena is secular or religious. As such, Marxist-Leninist dogma is a failure of nerve on the part of much of the world. What began as a social justice revolution ended in the atrophy of the human mind and will in a nineteenth-century economics and an inadequate critique of us and our religion. A proletarian freedom ended in a new and total elitist authoritarianism. In capitalist countries the failure to include the human dimension in the economic curve has led to crushing consumerism and an almost complete bypassing of the poor and an environment ravaged by 'economic progress'. An almost religious fervor for knowledge and the power it brings has given science and its practitioners an eery power over us and our future. The quest for degrees, seen most pitifully in the people of the Third World all but papering their walls with western diplomas, sends the gifted in a narcissistic search for a false self. And in religion, the failure of the imagination to conjure up the real misses God both in the poor and the rich. It makes us batten on old *formulae* in lieu of symbolling the religious existential, our fluxing a priori, anew. The failure of the religious imagination is rooted in the failure of religious nerve. We fear to confront the contemporary world. We feel inadequate and somewhat mediocre before the serried ranks of scientists and secular intellectuals; so much so that we have allowed the techniques of science to befuddle us. We have damaged the myth in performing false analysis. We have learned the technique of the secular imagination, but have forgotten that religious faith enriches its secular progenitor; instead, secularity has impoverished us religiously. We have gone in search of secular degrees and come home to work on our a prioris and those of the past with zeal and brilliance that dazzle us, blinding us to its sometime inadequacy to the task. We forget that when secularity damages healthy religious myth then *logos* has cast a shadow over *mythos*. To separate intellect and will from the imagination causes sensation (empiricism) without sensibility.

The highpoint of the secular imagination, the secular sensibility, is the synoptic view of the One, the True, and the Good, the classic transcendentals,which are the symbols of the human a priori. Philosophy has not given us this synoptic view for centuries because modernity, the emerging fragmented competence of the empirical method, protests against integralism in the name of the rationalization of every facet of human endeavor. This is the triumph of *logos* over *mythos*, of Appolo over Dionysus, of commerce over the love of wisdom (philosophy). I said earlier that philosophy is a failed religion in our day since modernity has placed religion in the back room and only allows philosophy room as a guardian over religion. Philosophy has offered no view of our a priori which was human and whole since it cannot come to grips with concepts such as Truth and Reality. It is in thralldom to science and its master, the empirical method. The secular imagination can work only if the religious imagination is healthy. That latter imagination began to fail when the two camps, Protestantism and Catholicism, drew the lines and refused to think very much irenically -- with the freedom of the transcendental a priori -- for four centuries. When religion fails to imagine the world, philosophy must fail also since its a priori, though secularly anterior to religion, is entitatively held on a human substrate constituted by a human existential whose sensibility is in process of being transmuted by a divine existential offering it no violence, but the fullness of its capacity for the infinite. The secular is finite since it is creature. The religious is creature which is infinite since God has willed it so. The secular, philosophical, imagination can only come to grips fully with the three transcendentals if religion works. We can't fault the failure of secularity without more trenchantly faulting the failure of the religious imagination to conjure up the symbols for man, woman, world and God. That brings us to the second moment, the religious imagination and the religious a priori as the core of method.

Endnotes for Chapter IV

Method: The First Moment

1.William F. Lynch, S.J., *Christ and Prometheus: A New Image of the Secular*, Notre Dame U. Press, 1978. The whole Lynch corpus well repays studying. See also his *Images of the Faith: An Exploration of the Ironic*. South Bend: U. of Notre Dame Press, 1973. I am heavily indebted to him for my notions of secularity and faith.
2.Ibid., pp. 40-71 passim.
3.Ernest Becker, *Revolution in Psychiatry, The New Understanding of Man*, London, Free Press, 1964, p. 155.
4. Marie Louise von Franz and James Hillman, *Lectures on Jung's Typology*, Zurich, Spring Publications, 1971, pp. 116-120 passim.

Chapter V

Method:

The Second Moment:
the Religious A Priori,
and Temperament

We can define the imagination as all the affective-cognitive powers of man and woman along with their whole life history and that of their communities brought to bear on the world in shaping and making it. Our agent intellect goes out to the world in sensibility, brings back the images the world affords it and abstracts from those percepts the universals which make for the idea, meaning and sanity. It is the intellect as imagination that makes sense of the percepts in its power to work on its allowing the world of matter to dominate it in its foray out beyond the safety of one's subjectivity. But, for the individual the job is too much on the secular level. So enter the religious imagination to make sense of its percepts. If the secular imagination can compose reality only so far before it runs into the limits of its blunted infinity, the religious imagination is also fraught with danger. The religious imagination fears to image the world lest it lose its soul in the process and so seeks the formulas and images of dogma and the Scriptures handed on by previous generations from their courageous and creative imaginings. But we cannot live on those imaginings alone. They shape us but are not definitive enough to feed us in our life in contemporary society. We must reimagine the secular world in order to see where its creaturehood is not. We must reimagine the faith in order to see where God and we are in relation to one another. Both the secular and religious images of the past and present are constitutive of our a priori, but neither of them is definitive. We must reimagine Self, world and God.

Thus, the second moment is the introduction of the religious faith a priori into method. We reimagine God and religion in order to live in the world. As an academic, I reimagine my secular self to be able to function as a human being. I criticize my categories, my images, in a philosophical sense in order to discern whether they are efficacious enough, creative and courageous enough, to allow my unconditionality and autonomy to produce the self and all its entails. I criticize them in a religious sense to allow God enough room to move around in me and me enough room to criticize him and appreciate him. The Psalms are filled with critiques of God: "How long, O Lord"; "Why are you sleeping?", etc. This religious moment is as aggressive as the secular moment because any question is a form of aggression, and religious questions are especially piquant aggressions.

In criticizing my religious a priori I am articulating it. Persons are always and only revealed in relation to another. Reflection is the ability to make the subject an other subject, what we have wrongly called an 'object', so that I might relate to it. I am finding myself in questioning myself in my religion and my religion in me. Am I wholesome or unwholesome, free or compulsed, angry or fearful? What do I believe? What does the Church teach? And how do I relate to it? Am I as free as I should be, or is dogma an ideology for me, a cudgel for beating down the emergent self of my neighbors? This is what I mean by the necessity of bringing the a priori into the methodology of the history of religions and the theology of religions. It is the self imagined, but is it secularly unconditioned and autonomous (the secular moment); and is it healthily conditioned and autonomous in the authority structure which is religion? Religious conditioning does not do away with secular unconditionality; our symbols do not make us symbols. We don't stand for anything else. We are not an infinite progression of masks and symbolic baubles. The buck stops at the Self. The a priori, the paradigm and the mask are the self only analogously. The self is , in a sense, created by its symbols, but it is always immeasurably greater than they are. But the self does not function without its a priori and its symbolic expressions. That is why we must, i) bring it into method -- we couldn't think without it; and ii) criticize it to purify it.

When we imagine ourselves we become that form: we are a 'mystical body' or a 'people' or 'children' or 'creatures'. Avery Dulles, S.J.'s *Models of the Church* is a popular classic depicting the a prioris or paradigmatic images the church has used down through the centuries to imagine itself for itself. (1) The image is produced by the church and, in turn, produces the church. Thus we see ourselves as institution, mystical body, sacrament, herald or servant. Our images give us a preferential option for the poor or for socialism or capitalism, for monarchy or democracy, depending on the age and circumstances.

In my own life I have had to deal with the church as institution, substituting, more and more, an image as mystical body in the fifties, then through criticism which saw that as mystical but triumphalist, as servant and pilgrim sinner holding itself out as helper to the world. I have gone from a heavily institutionalized view to two images, the mystical and the servant of the poor; polarities the twain of which are not yet meeting in me or in any large sense in the church, either. The secular image of objectivity has given way to one of subjectivity with understanding and fairness both to myself and others. I include my a priori and jettison epoche because such false objectivity is an impossible task for anyone, secular or religious, especially religious. There is nothing wrong with healthy subjectivity; it is destructive and perverse subjectivity, forcing others into one's own molds, that is the bugbear. Fairness and the critical mentality of my colleagues take care of the latter. Only I can see to the former.

The model I see as most useful in the history and theology of religions is that of pilgrim. We are simple people, travelling light, looking for something, bringing something; and looking more than bringing when it comes to studying other religions. But, as pilgrims, we cannot understand the other except in terms of our own a priori. If we have not only an autonomous secular and religious faith in the other and in his religion, that both are good, we will change for the better in coming to know him. As our a priori changes we change and the transcendent within changes. This means that God and the church and the self change in bringing our a priori to bear, our image as both servant and pilgrim, on the other. Our mystical image allows me to know Hinduism and Buddhism in their mysticism. Our institutional image does more harm than good in knowing Hinduism and Buddhism. Certainly there is the authority of the guru and the idea of Buddhism as a community, a sangham. But they are in no way like our popes, bishops and our idea of the institutional church. The ordination of buddhist bonzes is in no way like those in the Roman communion. The image of the priest-scholar as an *alter Christus* (another Christ) is so ponderous as to become burdensome in going out to our brothers and sisters in the other religion; it makes us lean too heavily towards converting the other rather than learning about him. Pilgrim allows a lighter touch to the scholar than does *sacerdos*. We must choose the right image for our time and place to do the job; choosing the image is the art of the method allowing one's symbol and mask to seek out the other's symbol and mask. This allows us to live in our world and to do things such as study others and make sense of them to both us and to themselves. If after we have studied Nagarjuna an authoritative Buddhist says, "Yes, that's him", our method has been successful. One should take no triumphalist pride in 'getting to' the heart of any religion, even one's own. It is a profound gift, one that frequently comes only after the humiliation of searing criticism.

Protestants had criticized our authoritarianism and obscurantism so well that it sent us hastening to their universities to study with them when Vatican II opened our eyes and said that they had something to say to us about us. Thus, the model or paradigm which flows out of the a priori has the reflexive function of creating that a priori in the sense of maintaining it; the classical definition of a cause is anything which brings something into existence or maintains it after its initial causation. To refrain from employing the a priori in any human endeavor would be to remove us from it as well, at most; or, at least, to the extent that we excised part of it, to that extent are we absent from it in our most human operations of knowing and loving. In this sense splitting the imagination faculty from the cognitive one is to lose one's sensibilities, the core of one's a priori allowing it to feel-know anything, but especially the self.

Thus this second moment allows the faith not only to compose reality, co-creating the religious person with the secular first moment, but it composes one as scholar of religion as well. One's secular human sensibilities are enhanced by the vision afforded by Revelation. With that sight we see people and things with God's eyes; it is the difference between knowledge, which is to know the causes of things, and wisdom, which is to know things in their causes, to see them against the full background of reality; which background not only includes God, no one 'includes' God, but sees him as the background and underground and overhead of our being. With this sensibility one can become the artist doing theology and the history and theology of religions I spoke of earlier. One can feel-know into both the self and into the self of others and their religion, which is always a self in relation to itself (as in Buddhism) or to the self in itself and as it resides in God (as it is in the religions of the West). This second moment of allowing religious faith to endow the imagination with the power to compose all reality for us situates us in the world, allowing us to live comfortably here. It is a full view giving us the responses to the deepest human questions; such as, where we come from, who we are, why we are here, where we are going, and are both God and our eschatological destiny worth it? Thus, fully composed as human through secular and religious criticism and the articulation (symbolization) it affords us, we are armed for the task of approaching our own or other religions as historian or theologian.

88

II

Method As Temperament and Style

Before moving on to the third and fourth moments of method, naming and hermeneutics, it is well for us to pause for a while on how temperament and style shape one's a priori and therefore one's mask. Thus, the shape of one's intellectual output will be, in large part, due to the way one lives one's life in the matter of his feeling and style. I have already said that feeling is a cognitive function, that one arrives at the felt-known in making one's ideas and masks. Here, we shall use as devices two methods for discerning the taxonomy of one's temperament. Hence, we shall offer an articulation of Jung's *Psychological Types* (1924) arrived at by David Keirsey and one of his students, Marilyn Bates.

We choose who we shall be in life -- the way we shall conduct ourselves psychologically -- , and this quite early on. Basically, Jung found that we are either extroverts or introverts (hereafter E and I, respectively). The extravert chooses to energize himself by engaging with people, whereas the introvert prefers to recharge the batteries by tending towards solitude. Extroverts like crowds and parties; introverts at parties choose one or two conversational partners and tend to leave early, leaving others with the impression that they are dull or 'snooty'. The extravert, therefore, is sociable, whereas the introvert is territorial, desiring space over people. [And, one's theology reflects this as a person-centered vs. a turf-centered -- an us vs. them, or right vs. wrong -] theology. In a crowd, introverts can actually be lonely. Though they enjoy people, they become drained quickly by them due to the intensity of their intimacy. (2) Extroverts derive intensity by interacting, so they may seem shallow to an introvert, though this is not the case. Each chooses intimacy in different ways. And, as scholars, each shapes the way he pursues his discipline differently. The introvert thinks out his thoughts fully before putting them down on paper. The extravert doesn't know what he is thinking until he says it. This makes it necessary for an extravert to rewrite much more than the introvert. I am an extravert and have written this piece five times already. The extravert's style is breezy, and seems to an introverted reader to be shallow. Sometimes it is, sometimes not. One shouldn't mistake style for content. The introvert may seem too tight to an extraverted reader. One should know oneself, one's temperament and living style to understand how he 'does' religion or anything else.

89

The side of one's character which is less favored is also less differentiated and less energized. It tends to be primitive and undeveloped. For instance, when an introvert tries to become the life of the party or write in a breezy manner he seems quirky, strange to his viewers and readers. In the general population there are 75 percent extroverts and 25 percent introverts. The key words for the extraverted and the introverted are sociability over against territoriality, breadth over depth, externality as opposed to internality, extensive as opposed to intensive, multiple relationships over limited ones; profligacy with one's energy as opposed to conservation; and interest in external happenings as opposed to interest in what is going on inside one. (3) Thus, all this shapes everything one is and does, including one's theology.

But, even more important and telling about the way we think than introversion and extraversion are what Keirsey and Bates -- and many modern Jungians -- call intuition and sensation (hereafter, N and S , respectively). Those who prefer sensation would see themselves as 'practical' and conservative, while the intuitive person would describe himself as innovative (4) and others would label him as progressive in politics and religion. Keirsey says that these two preferred styles are the sources of much misunderstanding and even vilification between the people -- and I would add groups -- which practice them. I say groups, since some ethnic groups and some religions seem to prefer the one over the other. For instance, Islam is radically conservative even to saying that 'reformation' as a category belongs to Christianity, not to Islam. Muslims go back to the way things were, not to the way things are today. The Qur'an determines the way things must be, always. Thus, N's and S's have a difficult time getting along with other since, at first blush, they don't like each other. Their preferred styles put the other type off. It might be well to mention here that Cardinal Ratzinger, head of the Vatican's Congregation for the Doctrine of the Faith, is an S, while Hans Kung, whose theology he deplores is an N, as are so many of the liberation theologians like Jon Sobrino, Leonardo Boff, etc., all of whom have come under his fire. The S (sensation-preferring person) wants facts, plain and simple. His faith is in this and his own experience. Keirsey describes him as 'earth-bound', grounded in rock-hard reality. He likes history, personal or communitarian. He wants to know what happened, not what might happen or might have happened. He likes factual history, not hermeneutics. He loves creeds over systematic and speculative theology. He likes what the group has decreed in faith and morals and politics, not what it might have done or might do in the future. He brooks the intuitive not at all when this type says, "Yes, but it would look so good to do it this way." His retort verbally and in writing is likely to be, "It has been this way, and no other way is acceptable." Thus the two can't stand each other as persons or scholars. Sensation-preferrers like the factual and make wonderful phenomenologists since they don't miss a thing. They tend to be weak methodologically when it comes to stepping back and saying, What does all this mean? For them, appearance is the reality. As Catholics, they tend to be the type of theologian who loves dogmatic formulae, moral dicta, rubrics. They tend to be fundamentalistic about whatever the group has decreed and depart from it only at the cost of great grief. They would be classed as non-historically orthodox in the sense that they haven't the modern sense of historical and cultural specificity. By this I mean that they are bound by what has been said and done and want it done and said in exactly that way, finding great difficulty in the exegete's facility with finding out the spirit of the decree or fact over the letter. The intuitive-based person found it easy to accept historicity as a basis for scholarship and churchmanship. He found it easy to go with the attitude that found what the decree or dogma intended over what it said, with the meaning behind the scriptural formula, with *mythos* over *logos*, therefore. The S person is Appolonian in his scholarly endeavors and the N person more Dionysian.

The N person loves metaphor and vivid imagery. He daydreams, likes poetry, preferring fantasy and fiction to history and biography. The possible attracts him over the actual. For him the is is just for openers; he loves what might be or might have been. Facts easily bore him. He is less good at phenomenology than the S person since he misses things, taking the ball and running to speculation with one fact when there is a whole *Gestalt* to be taken with it. This latter reaction drives the S person to distraction. The N person goes with a hunch, where the S person distrusts it. Freud was the quintessential N person in this regard. The N person loves to characterize the world and history as dynamic while the S person sees it as a static entity. Hegel and Friedrich Engels, as well as Charles Darwin and Aristotle and Aquinas are N's, while Ronald Reagan and Margaret Thatcher are S's. The N, therefore, is a romantic in history and theology, whereas the S person is classical. The N person is open to mysticism, the S person says that mysticism begins in mist and ends in schism. These two will, therefore, face their own and other religions in somewhat radically different ways, coming up with differing and often contradictory readings of the same texts or religious phenomenon. The N person thinks that things can always be better. When he is working in committee he will keep things open to the extreme discomfort of the S person who wishes to bring things to a head when he sees a consensus. For the N person, in a sense, reality is an affront. It can always be better; fine tune it. The N person doesn't like to finish projects. He is wonderful at coming up with the initiating idea, and is quite happy to let others put 'wheels under it'. He sees the S as a plugger, a bit of a bore. The S person views the N as a lightweight. The American military would call the N a 'feather merchant'. S persons tend to be administrators and militaristic. In theology, process theologians tend to be N's. Unreconstructed Thomists, whose derivative and somewhat incorrect view of Aquinas infuriated Luther and formed generations of Catholic seminarians down to Vatican II, are S's. Transcendental Thomists like Karl Rahner and Bernard Lonergan are N's. Karl Barth was an S, while Tillich was an N.

The S person values experience over the N's hunches; the conservative wisdom of the past over the progressive possibilities of the present and future; the real over the possible; fact over speculation. Buzzwords for the S person are actual, down-to-earth, no-nonsense, fact, practical, and sensible. He is the quintessential empiricist, in this regard. The N person loves to hear words like possible, fascinating, fantasy, fiction, ingenious and imaginative. In the U.S., 75 percent of the population would prefer S, while 25 would be N types. (5) The genius of American philosophy is in its pragmatic and utilitarian S-type school of men like James, Pierce, Mead and Dewey, not the intuitive N-type philosophy of Descartes, Berkeley, Leibniz, Hegel, Marx, Heidegger, Nietzsche and Heidegger. It has been said that *the* religion of Americans is Methodism, with its emphasis on doing over dogma, on ethics over speculation. If so, this is an S-type theology over the N-type of high Anglicans and Roman Catholics, both of which latter have either been seen as or acted against as 'foreign' to our *Zeitgeist*, from time to time.

The next set of binary pairs is thinking versus feeling. One who bases his decisions on an impersonal basis, on the logic or principle of the thing, is a thinking T type. But a person who decides on how an issue will affect people or by what value is being served is called a P type. The scholar who is more comfortable with the logic of an issue will tend to go with that style towards making his scholarly choices and conclusions. The scholar who is more comfortable with the personalistic will tend to go that way and be less easy with the heteronomous nature of a highly structured, rule-bound religion. In both Protestantism and Catholicism today the F person dominates the progressives while the T person does the conservatives. Thus a pattern seems to be emerging. Conservatives today will tend to be ST's, while liberals will be NF's. This means that their a prioris, their paradigms and masks, in a word, their whole lifestyle and scholarly style, is shaped by this psychological preference. Anthropology shapes it all.

The only sexual difference in all the Jungian types will be found here. Six out of ten women decide as F's, while six out of ten men decide issues as T's, that is, on the basis of the logic of it. F's like to malign T's for being cold-hearted, for "living in their heads" and can quite frequently win the day with this manipulative ploy if they are somewhat authoritative persons. For their part, T's easily put down F's for being 'weak sisters', 'bleeding hearts', 'wishy washy', emotional or illogical, for being too fuzzy to take an intellectual stand. (6) When a scholar, by dint of being stampeded by his or her colleagues due to either fad or emotionality, has to make a decision in a way not according to his style, he frequently botches it. T's have developed their logical side, and F's their personalistic style. The Roman Catholic church was a T church in the way it did its moral thinking until the personalism of the fifties filtered into the Second Vatican Council. Then morality became more person-centered than it had for centuries. Bernard Haering's epoch-making book on charity as the key to moral theology caused a paradigm shift in a whole generation of young thinkers, with profound effects, for instance, during the controversy on birth control that anteceded and succeeded the 1968 encyclical of Paul VI called *Humanae Vitae*, his final pronouncement on birth control. His was a decision made by an INT, who had taken heavy advice from theological S's -- tradition-based, conservative, scholars. These temperament styles shape what we can see and what we can do. They shape our blind spots and cause lacunae. They create intellectual communities, those who share paradigms, and thus fashion the identities of individuals and whole religions. One is a Protestant, for instance, because one's stylistic forebears rejected the Roman Catholic monarchic style of running the church. They preferred a style more open to giving power to the emerging middle class, one diffusing or even atomizing authority -- depending on the religious communion. Thus, the way one's communion shaped one determined in large part how one would do one's theology. Catholics saw an umbilical link between the successor of Peter and Christ. The pope is seen as the vicar of Christ. The way we do our theology, therefore is largely shaped by this intuition, by this hierophany: the power of the papacy derives, ultimately, from God. And one can tell an S Catholic that it was set up this way and that way because of human necessity and is reformable, but that will not change him or her. An S is an S because of his religious and secular a priori, the one feeds and shapes the other. Many a convert to Catholicism before the Council came because he was an S and wanted things to be ironed out on the basis of past facts, not present needs. Again, these temperamental styles are choices and become habitual tendencies, one is not compulsed to go one way or the other. But if one goes against one's habitual style, strange things happen. The opposing style is undeveloped and quirky. Further, one may feel that one has 'sold out' one's principles or one's very self, by departing from one's chosen style, which style begins in infancy, not graduate school. We learn our a prioris and E's and I's, etc. at our mother's knee. When one shifts to one's shadow -- undeveloped -- side the results in scholarship and even life style can become bizarre. Think of the colleagues we have known whose radical shift in thought produced not only oddness in subsequent behavior, but precipitated zany or even disastrous life decisions. Whether the thought fathered the behavior or vice versa is immaterial. What is relevant is that conversion leaves one with a vacuum which is frequently filled by unanticipated devils.

When faced with an issue or problem to be solved a T type scholar will resonate with words such as objective, principle, policy, laws, criteria and firmness. An F type scholar responds positively to such words as subjective, values, social values, extenuating circumstances, intimacy and persuasion. T's love words like justice, categories, standards, critique, and analysis, while F's prefer humane, harmony, good or bad, appreciate, sympathy and devotion. T's tend to be better at argumentation than F's, while F's are adept at appealing to emotion to win the day with themselves or others. The U.S. population is split down the middle percentage-wise between T's and F's. (7)

The last binary pair in the Jungian system as advanced by Keirsey and Bates is judging versus perceiving [J or P, respectively]. When making a decision or settling an affair demanding a solution do I prefer to keep my options open or do I call for cloture the moment I see sufficient grounds for making a decision? The type wanting to keep things open is a perceiving type P and the type persistently seeing a sense of urgency demanding cloture is a judging type J. A P type feels restless when he has to make a decision. He feels trapped by it. He wants to see more data. A scholarly type of this sort will be ABD (finished with his Ph.D. studies, All But Dissertation) for a long time because he has to take just one more course or read one more article before he can put pen or word processor to paper. When a person with a high tendency to be a P person is also an introvert (I), he wants things fully thought out before he can get it down, before he can articulate it. This person feels nothing but agony when writing. It is never perfect. An E (extravert), N (intuitive), F (feeler), J (judger) revels in getting it down the first time. But then he wants to leave it. The intuitive person hates to edit himself; deplores the necessity to finish a project. It bores him and gives him the feeling that he has limited himself and sold himself out just by getting something on paper and closing it out. The so-called high J (a person with a strongly developed tendency to call for cloture) won't feel easy until things are done, over, finished, brought to a head so that it can be precedent for the future. When a scholar is an STJ he will tend to be conservative because of his S paradigm, wants things settled on the basis of principle -- that is, the way the wise have done it before, or always -- and wants it done quickly so that things won't get out of hand. Such a person comes on to an NFP as if he were wearing wooden shoes and clopping all over the place in them. The NFP wants more delicatesse. The T-ness of the T person wants an elegant principle; his S-ness will settle for just the facts, wanting a good principle; and his J-ness might tend to step on toes to get the 'bloody mess' cleaned up and get on with life. The NFP hemorrhages psychic energy when faced with this type of scholarly situation. He wants to do his canvas using broad strokes of the brush, deploring the need to get down to the finer details, which an S person would want. And he wants to do it over and over, finally leaving it unfinished, trusting in another scholar, the sheer goodness of things or of God, to bring it to a happy conclusion.

Thus, a J type shares the so-called Protestant work ethic. A P type is somewhat Catholic, as the Irish and Italians are seen by those who don't know them: that is, as fun-loving and somewhat feckless. The J will prepare far in advance of doing the scholarly job. He will keep at it, rewriting it until it is perfect and then clean up the jots and tittles afterwards. The P plunges in, trusting to his talent, he doesn't like to edit and deplores completions. Since the last skill to come to a scholar-writer is that of editing himself, the NFP has a hard time 'killing the little babies' -- one's bon mots, which might have begun a work, but which have to go in order to get at just what the writer is trying to say. The J type's paradigm as censor is constantly admonishing him, "What are you trying to say?" It makes scholarship a torment while doing it, but gives peace and ease at completion. A P is never happy with his intellectual creations since he thinks that they could have been done better by doing them this way or that. P's love to play with their work and seem to J's to be shallow or lightweight. This is not necessarily so. NFP's are extremely creative and follow the muse where it takes them, frequently blazing new trails. STJ's deplore new trails and reject the work of those who make them as departures from tradition, as illogical, as insightful but incomplete. J's describe P's as indecisive, procrastinating, aimless, feckless, obscurantist, and just plain sophistic, with their playing around with things intellectual. P's deplore working with J's since they feel pressured, think that the others jump to conclusions, feel that they are task-oriented at the risk of hurting the project (NFP's keep feeling that J's hurt 'their' people -- they tend to take responsibility for people, even when, especially when, it isn't there). STJ's, for their part, take responsibility for the truth, and P's censure them for letting the chips fall where they may, even if people get hurt in the process.

Buzzwords that warm the cockles of J hearts -- and they make excellent administrators, since they make conclusions without crushing people -- are words like settled, decided, fixed, plan ahead, take control of one's life, cloture, front-loaded, goal-specific, goal-intensive, urgency, deadlines, getting the show on the road. P people are warmed by such words as pending, gather more data, flexibility, play it by ear, open-ended -- they love that one --, emergent, tentative, what deadline?, something good will turn up, let's wait and see. Like T's and F's, P's and J's split the U.S. population right down the middle. P's who are in charge of a project, tend to become high J's, calling for cloture quickly. It is a reversion to their undeveloped side, for some reason that defies explanation. But the psychologists have found that, since this side is undeveloped, they tend to be rather heavy-handed when they assume control of a situation. When they are NFP's they are so people-oriented that they want to preserve 'their' people from hurt and thus, in their liberalism, become as autocratic as those whom they wanted to throw out of office or positions of churchly authority in the first place. (8) Their psychology can thrust them beyond where they would go intellectually, when in a crisis situation.

There are four basic alliances that Keirsey delineates: SPs, SJ's, NP's and NF's. He calls the SP combination the Dionysian Temperament. One can have an ISTP, and ESTP, An ISFP, and an ESFP. What these four have in common is that an SP won't be bound or obligated by duty, any power or any god. These latter are of secondary importance. What is primary is freedom. One must squeeze as much enjoyment as each day offers, tomorrow doesn't come. Hence, SP's are impulsive and want to be that way. In fact, they feel guilty if they aren't impulsive. When he faces his work, the SP scholar doesn't like goals. When he feels cornered he tends to leave the project for another one. SP's don't prepare for a project by practicing, they just sit down and 'do' it. They are excessively action-oriented, a fact which may be mistaken for discipline by careless readers of their work. They grind out the work as if it were on a mimeo machine. [A colleague writes so prolifically that it has been said that he has no unpublished thought.] Some call this desire to do a 'function lust', "a function for action without the necessity for rules or practice." I have found that this type abounds in the ministry, and when he becomes a scholar one has to watch it that he doesn't come in front of his guns. He can be a foeman worthy of the best steel. He thrives on

96

crisis, and where there is none he will tend to create one. He is constantly testing the limits of his and his group's freedoms. He is a gadfly. He is courageous in a crisis and responds with characteristic generosity and verve. He hates dullness.

He rankles before the deity since he imposes constraints on one's freedom. Symbols bore him, so he tends not to like systematics or hermeneutics. He is an activist. He loves gadgets and tools, the latter becoming an extension of himself. He is optimistic, cheerful, light-hearted and loves fun. He is charming and witty in conversation. He knows all the jokes and stories going around and regales his auditors with them whether they want them or not; usually they are so interesting or funny that, willy nilly, one listens with rapt attention. In scholarship, they become the supreme innovators, the prime-movers of the social gospel, moral rearmament, liberal or conservative causes. They can't stand the status quo. Like the Irishman landing on a desert isle their first words are, "Whatever the government, I'm against it." And that, just to keep things lively. When they are involved in writing about social justice one should beware of their charm and the verve with which they throw themselves in the cause. They won't be there in five years. Where are the hippies? In Larchmont counting their CD's. Whatever ties he makes he keeps. He is fiercely loyal to his friends, family and religion. He joins the Marines and the right wing of the Republican party, the liberal wing of the Democrats and likes his religion hot. He will give away anything that a brother or sister needs. He is egalitarian to the core. As scholar, he is known more for advocacy than profundity. But he is not to be scanted. When he has an abundance of intelligence, his talents can cover up a paucity of research with a profusion of loosely joined facts. He knows the darndest things. In scholarship he trusts as much to talent and luck and the sheer goodness of his enterprises as research. (9)

The type that longs for duty as much as the SJ deplored it is the Epimethean Temperament. Named after the brother of Prometheus who married Pandora and stuck with her through thick and thin. There are four possible combinations: the ISFJ, ESFJ, ISTJ, and the ESTJ. Thirty eight percent of the U.S. population shares the SJ preference. In the face of adversity he seeks out the moral imperative to shield him. Thus, he is in constant search of shoulds and oughts as talismans against the surds of life. In scholarship, therefore, he is a moralizer, no matter what field he takes up. He needs to belong since he can't abide being an outsider. He must give and finds difficulty in accepting any gift. He must care for people and things and not be cared for. He is out of touch with his needs and in touch with everyone else's. He loves schools since he wants to learn what must be done. Having learned it, he loves to run schools so he can tell others what they, too, must do. He is the perpetual parent. Where the SP was an epicure, the SJ is a Stoic and binds himself to be a puritan and a workaholic. He must have hierarchy as much as the SP demanded equality. One can see how this would work out with Catholics and Protestants and what they would uphold in their scholarly pursuits. And one can see, just as easily, how an SP would be a maverick in a Catholic community while an SJ would be one in a liberal Protestant one. The SJ demands rules to guide society and theological method. He deplores an intuitive approach. He shuts down the metaphor as a locus for theological insight. He demands that one's place in the hierarchy be earned. For him, there is no room for nepotism.

His desire is to be useful. His scholarship, therefore, will hove towards the 'how to' type books since one knows the hows and wherefores when one knows the rules of things, which rules he learned and updates for the untutored.The core of his personality is that he is a fosterer and maintainer of the society to which he belongs. As churchperson and scholar he will be a conservator and strive to let his auditor and reader know what must be preserved to maintain himself and his church in being. He feels incapable of refusing any request made on his generosity, feeling that if he doesn't do it no one will. He wants power so that he can maintain the academy or church and hand it on to others when he is finished with his task. He both deplores and resists change as betraying the imperatives of his nature and the group to which he claims membership. He feels that the only way to freedom is inequality, hierarchy doth make one free. One must submit to authority, and his desire is to become the authority to which one submits, not out of a desire to aggrandize himself, but out of a fervor to maintain and pass on the ideals of his group. He is constantly in search of the young or old, the one to nurture and the other to preserve them from the outrages of change. His zeal makes him peculiarly vulnerable to depression and nervous exhaustion when he feels that he is insufficiently appreciated for his efforts. This combination comprises thirty eight percent of the U.S. population. (10)

The next combination, the Promethean Temperament, joins N with T. These Prometheans desire power, the fire of the gods. They want to know the laws of nature so as to control it. This is a peculiarly modern and post-modern trait in scholarship, though only twelve percent of the population chooses it as a temperamental style. What they desire and demand of themselves, their educators, their colleagues, and especially their betters is competence. The four aims of science are control, understanding, prediction and explanation. Keirsey says, "Scratch an NT, find a scientist." One might just as easily say this of this type of theologian. He or she is the quintessential systematician or hermeneut. What he wants is skill, ability, ingenuity: in a word, repertoire. In the extreme, he is an addict at storing up wisdom. He is an encyclopedist, storing up knowledge, forever taking courses, piling up insights like a squirrel, against the intellectual winter. Where the SP sees ability and performance as ends the NT sees performance as the means and ability as the goal. He wants to be able to do and does so that he becomes better at doing his discipline. He does his craft as a perpetual set of finger exercises, never getting to an opus magnum, but always piling up wonderful little essays. Karl Rahner was an NT. His corpus is a series of essays, *Theological Investigations* is the title of the several volumes of his corpus. In them he followed a theme and did essays towards its accomplishment. Lonergan was an SP, melding the great insights into a few wonderful books. Mircea Eliade is an SP, taking his originating insight on the terror of history, and applying it all over the place; it was ability in the service of performance.

Of all the styles, the NT is the most aware of himself, constantly critical of his performance because his ability needs work. And when anyone criticizes him he looks the more easily and quickly at the critic's credentials than at his criticism. He rejects even the best authorities, since the best can err. He seems arrogant as a consequence, but it isn't necessarily so. He wants both that the statements made by colleagues to be those of competents and that their competence stand the test of analysis. He seems individualistic to the extreme. But this is not necessarily so. He wishes to check everyone's credentials and their statements by the high canons he sets for himself. He is constantly haunted by the thought that he may be a failure, or that a project in which he is engaged might be futile. Consequently, and especially when he is an NTP, he goes into action only with the greatest reluctance. He knows everything about his subject, but never feels that he knows enough. He conveys contradictory messages to his colleagues and students: that he expects little from them, and this is since they don't know much and therefore can't do much. The contradictory message is that, even though they can't do much, they had better be up to the high standard that he sets for himself. He puts himself and the whole of the academy in a double bind. This tends to make his students and colleagues withdraw from him, thinking he is constantly talking down to them, when, all along, he is talking to himself, giving himself little pep talks: "Come on, get on with it. Get up to standard, you dolt. You can't teach anyone anything because you don't know enough. Don't open your mouth until you have something to say." He is hard to live with. He can hardly abide himself. For him, more than for any of the other combinations, his work is his pleasure. He has no other life but his work. His lust is not the function lust of the SP, rather, it is a knowledge lust. He wants to know the law for everything. He is, to put it vulgarly, a "hermeneutics freak." He easily cuts himself off from the workaday world due to the monomanaical drive to know his discipline. He lives in the proverbial ivory tower and disdains the rest of the world as unworthy of his attentions. He moves from competency in one field or aspect of it to another field, constantly throwing himself new challenges. But, he never leaves off developing the skills, even of disciplines long since mastered. The great scripture scholar William Foxwell Albright of Johns Hopkins said that he knew twenty eight languages. Many of those whom he trained rank among the greatest scholars and NT's of this writers acquaintance. The NT is so absorbed at figuring out the import of what is happening that he misses the event that is happening. Thus he tends to make personal alliances on the basis of too little feeling because this function is undeveloped. And he tends, in later life, to regret these alliances with colleagues or even, and especially, members of the opposite sex. This insensitivity to the feeling content of colleagues or loved ones tends to make them sense that he doesn't know that they exist. In his scholarship, he emphasizes *logos* over *mythos*, and thought over feeling, seeing the discursive as the only way to truth. This makes him particularly dangerous when doing a religion with a heavy mystical content, such as Roman Catholicism, Islam, Hinduism or Buddhism. When apprised of this blind spot NT's are so bewildered that they seldom counter with a riposte. They are oblivious to their insensitivity and lack of developed sensibility. (11)

The last of the temperaments is the Appolonian, or the NF, intuitive-feeler. This is one whose life goal almost defies description. Basically, what he seeks is the extraordinary. The other combinations understand the goals of their counterparts, but to the NF sees them all as inauthentic. For him the only goal is *becoming*. He wants to actualize himself, to be what he is inside, what he is meant to be, what nature destined him to be when he is courageous and goes on the solitary pilgrim's path to find that Self. So the NF wanders the solitary path of perfection, craving meaning in his life. But more, he must have his meaningful life known and appreciated. Seeing life as a drama in which each moment is significant unto itself, he will live it to the full and give its fullness to others for nothing, seeking no reward but only that others *know* that he is out there, living and giving freely of what he is, of what he has become. He is the quintessential writer. NT's might be better systematic thinkers and scientific writers in the empirical disciplines and in theology than the NF's, but the flair with which the NF communicates makes him or her by far the most influential person in our culture. Only twelve percent of the U.S. population is comprised of NF's, but they are the teachers, the novelists, the influential philosophers, the psychiatrists, physicians and clergypersons. They move the nation by serving it. They are nurturers by nature. When they communicate they change people and institutions. Martin Buber was such. Thomas Merton was an NF and changed our perception of the holy and the good when he got down to writing of how God exists in our sinfulness. Reinhold Neibuhr was an NF, constantly putting his intuitions of justice down to change a whole generation of young Americans. The great novelists and poets are NF's. What NF's seek in all that they do is intimacy. When they communicate in writing, therefore, they are seeking intensity and intimacy with their readers. What they look for in religion is intimacy. They want the God in the text, rite or building. They are the quintessential personalists, but they enflesh it when they write. Their verve takes the reader with them in search of his own self even as the writer quests for that most elusive being within himself.

As an intellectual, the NF can be a butterfly, going from flower to flower in search of his goal. Thus, he seems lightweight to NT's, who demand a rigor and discursive competence which is beyond the NF psychologically. It isn't that they aren't intelligent enough to have it, but that it does them violence when they have to attain it. NF's who do a good Ph.D. have a particularly hard time in graduate school since they are forced to develop the T side of their nature, the dark side which is undeveloped, undifferentiated. They find it fatuous to footnote an intuition. They love to flit from project to project, taking what they want from it, leaving it when they have satisfied their personal quest. As such, they find it difficult to finish anything. But when they undertake a commitment, they do it with a vengeance, demanding of colleagues their own high standards.

Keirsey calls them Appolonians since, like that god who symbolized the ambivalence or *chiaroscuro* of the Greek mindset, the NF will find it equally good to seek the heights of perfection and the depths of darkness. One thinks of the young Rimbaud, seeking God by going through the depths of depravity so that he might become a seer. The essence of the NF's is that they depreciate abstraction. What they want is a personal relationship. When they write, they do to engage themselves as much as their reader with persons as they typify ideals. Whatever they do in the healing professions or the academy it is to influence and change people. They are idealists seeking the heavens on earth as well as in the firmament. (12)

Thus, both the secular and religious a prioris are shaped by these paradigmatic combinations. And, in turn, these paradigms shape both the individual and his or her culture or religion. When the scholar comes to do theology or any form of religious studies, it is well that he be aware of his own a priori as well as that of the culture or religion on which he works. These are not only the styles of individuals, they describe cultures and languages as well. When they describe languages they say what the language will permit and what it will not, what it will allow one to see of its a priori, and what will remain hidden. The masks of our culture and religions, therefore, are styles, telling their stories as they obscure them. Some styles are more submissive to certain temperaments and certain religious predispositions or communions, and some prove resistant by their very nature. N's don't find S's easy to understand and vice versa. An extraverted style eludes the introvert, and vice versa. Each side of the four binary pairs indicates that the preferred style is differentiated and developed, but the other side is dark and undifferentiated. When that side comes out as mask, it is inauthentic in both individuals and groups, especially religious groups. As such, the shadow side is a sign, whereas the developed and preferred side is one's symbol when well done. But even in one's preferred side, both for individuals and groups, one has to ask, is this the best that he, she or they could and have done -- is this its symbol, its mask, its truth -- or is it merely a botched job, an arbitrary sign?

Endnotes for Chapter V
Method:
The Second Moment: The Religious A Priori
and Temperament

1. Avery Dulles, *Models of the Church*, Garden City: Doubleday, 1978.
2. David Keirsey and Marilyn Bates, *Please Understand Me: An Essay on Temperament Styles*. Del Mar, Ca. Prometheus Nemesis Books, 1978, pp. 14f.
3. Ibid, p. 16.
4. Ibid.
5. Ibid., pp. 18f.
6. Ibid., pp. 20f.
7. Ibid., pp. 21f.
8. Ibid., pp. 23f.
9. Ibid., pp. 30-39 passim.
10. Ibid., pp. 39-47 passim.
11. Ibid., pp. 47-51 passim.

Chapter VI

Method:
The Third and Fourth Moments

I

The Third Moment:
Naming

The process of facing up to any religion begins per se by addressing oneself to the writings, rites or sacred edifices of that religion. In Nagarjuna's Buddhism, for instance, we would have to look to the writings of Nagarjuna and an authoritative Buddhist practicing Buddhism in his spiritual line , D.T. Suzuki, to interpret him. In addition to this we might want to go to one who understood Indian spirituality in general, T.R.V. Murti, to gain background information. Then we would look to the short history of Buddhist art to see how Buddhists have symbolled their faith architectonically and iconographically. From the original and his interpreters in books and art we would then begin to pick up bits and pieces. This is the phenomenological moment of the process. The individual bits of Nagarjuna would be placed against a generalized Buddhist background. If any bit seemed to relate to another they would be placed together. Slowly we began to see a pattern emerging. When a pattern became discernible we looked for a name for it. Naming is the high point of phenomenology. It brings the bits together into something usable, meaningful. It is a choosing between a sign and a symbol because one has come to know the extrinsic and arbitrary from the intrinsic and necessary. Here, it is essential to remember that patterns interplay with each other. They move and dance. They don't stay put. Don't expect Christ or the Buddha to be static. People aren't static. They move and change constantly. And because religions are the interplay of people with one another and with some concept of the Ultimate, expect to see the bits and pieces fashioning themselves in a never ending floating mosaic. The names we assign the patterns might have to change in mid stream, but that is alright. The thing is to be aware that the object is changing and to reflect on the change it demands in one's own thinking and feeling.

Taking the bits and pieces of Nagarjuna's thoughts on dialectics and mysticism we find that his dialectics were a tool for "blowing the mind", reducing it to impotence before the experience of Nothingness which opens one up to Nirvana. Thus, he is telling us that philosophy will get one nowhere; that it is in the midst of one's darkness, in the midst of one's endless lives which the Buddhists call samsara, that one finds Nirvana. Thus the philosophical bits and pieces didn't make us end up by naming the religion of Nagarjuna as a philosophy which transforms one -- as did Frederick Streng in his book Nothingness. Rather, our conclusions are that Nagarjuna's religion is an experience-based one and that discursive reasoning -- dialectics -- in no way lead one to the transformation sought in Nirvana. Nirvana happens on its own. The transcendent has no hand holds. We serve it. Yoga and Buddhist asceticisms are not the efficient causes of Nirvana, merely its dispositive cause. They prepare the field for the seeds of contemplation and nirvana. Thus, the telling feature of our study would be the Buddhist praxis of meditation and contemplation, not Buddhist logic. What appears to be a philosophy of nihilism in Nagarjuna's concept of Nothingness is a very positive mystical experience which is salvific for the practitioner. Nirvana is thus to be found in the midst of samsara because the religious experience tells one so.

In many ways this is paralleled by contemporary western Christian secular theology where Jesus is to be found in the quintessentially human, the workaday world; this is the 'Jesus, and him alone' theme deriving from the Transfiguration narratives. If Jesus is the paradigm of God and we share his life, then the human is the medium of God in our lives. The holy is coterminous with the profane in the sense that the divine existential comes to us in the rites of water, bread, oil, human covenant, even, and especially, in human failure, and on and on. Nagarjuna's thought crystallized much of my own thoughts on the secular and the holy in my own faith. I use the phrase 'Christian secular theology' advisedly. The secularity of things, of us humans, is our frame. The frame puts order into what we see without drawing attention to itself. It is there, but unseen. The first step in 'seeing' the bits and pieces is to see the frame in which the bit to be studied sits. Frame circumscribes the Gestalt, it tells us that something is a whole not to be disturbed. We may analyze it, but to remove it does the whole such violence that it might destroy it. Thus, a frame is the device which gives place, and therefore meaning, to what is studied. Again, it is to be remembered that what we study has coordinates within its frame. To take a coordinate from one picture and line it up with a look-alike from another is to invite disaster. This is what I mean. In the New Testament, we are told that the price of our redemption was blood. In another place we are told that God demanded the death of his Son to save us. These are two metaphors, two non-discursive symbols -- to draw on Susan K. Langer's symbolology -- not meant to be strung together like pearls on a string. One doesn't derive a syllogism from metaphors. One cannot, therefore, coordinate bit A from system 1a with a look-alike, bit A, from system 2a and get anything theologically meaningful. When, for instance, one talks of Christian salvation and sees something like it in Pure Land Buddhism, one would make a mistake by lining them up as coordinates in a system like a theology of religions. Salvation in Christianity goes along with a Fall, a redemptive death, the historical incarnation of God -- the only God --, and a resurrection of that God-man from the dead. In Buddhism, there is no Fall, no incarnation, no resurrection. The cosmic Buddha is not historical, the earthly Buddha is. I could go on, but I think my meaning is clear.

What I am saying is that naming depends on first defining the frame of reference in order to see the bit studied in its matrix, which word alludes to a thing's place as being its mother. To rip it from its place in order to derive meaning is to, literally, bastardize it. If one cannot bowdlerize a text without doing it damage then neither can one pick one item from column A of one religion and another from column B of another and make sense of either. For instance, Rudolf Otto and Keiji Nishitani take pleasure and finding meaning in comparing the work and mysticism of Meister Eckhardt with the religious experience of the Hindu Shankara and Buddhist Emptiness, respectively. In the companion volume to this work I shall demonstrate that this is a faulty comparative method a principio. Eckhart's experience and the writings which bruited them about in the Christian community as being something Christian were condemned by the church as not being a Christian mysticism; and this condemnation has not been overturned by later generations of thinkers. A religion has the right and duty to say what is orthodox and what is not, what is itself and what is something other. If Otto and Nishitani wish to say that his experience was akin to those of the Hindu and Buddhist contemplatives, that is well and good and may be so. But to say that authentic Hindu and Buddhist experiences are either the same or analogous with authentic theistic Christian experience is not correct. It seems to me that to say any more than that the experiences are real experiences, which all were, and that they may well be identical is alright. To say that Hindu or Buddhist mysticism is Christian mysticism is an assertion, at times brilliantly adduced, but at no time demonstrated.

Secondly, just as no one gives him or herself a name, but receives if from one's parents, so the names we are looking for in this phenomenological parental moment of baptism is to be given by its relationship with the 'siblings' in its matrix. How the piece interacts within its field determines its name. When Mircea Eliade saw that the Polynesian phenomenon called *mana* was a manifestation of other-worldly power he called it a kratophany, a manifestation of power. When we have seen a phenomenon acting in its own field as the bit we are studying is acting in its field we can name it with a universal name if there is one, or we can coin a name for it. The trap in all this is to move directly from the name to the moment of meaning and to impose meaning that doesn't jibe with the theological context of the phenomenon. By this I mean that earlier practitioners of religious studies saw divine births and deaths in religions antedating Christianity and, by using form criticism, imposed the dynamics of myth on them. The inference they drew was that Christ's 'divine death and rebirth' was of the same nature as the mythological -- read, non-historical, fictional -- deaths and rebirths of nature religions. Meaning derives from within the frame, not from outside it. One may draw universals, but only by avoiding doing violence to the religion in question. If the people believe it, it is so. What the religious imagination composes is reality. We have come far enough to know that one definition of reality has little to do with the real. 'Reality' is an abstract noun; the real is not abstract, and it is both like and unlike what we create from it and call it knowledge. As I said earlier, science knows, finally, that the viewer changes the real just by viewing it and naming it. Science also knows that what is 'out there' cannot be embraced by the abstract noun 'reality'. The real is concrete, empiricism taught us that. But no universal that we know embraces it all. So no one knows reality *in toto*; that is, no one can draw up a definition that holds in every instance.

The trick to naming is the same trick that a novelist must learn in practicing his craft. One must let one's character speak for himself. A creation takes on a life of its own. To impose words on one's character in a given situation, a *Gestalt*, is to do violence to it. It is like eisegesis is to scripture studies. It is a misuse of one's a priori. One creates, but then the creation tells us what it is and what it wants to say. It defines itself, in other words. We do not define it. Allowing it to define itself demands acute sensitivity to what is going on in the text, rite, etc., and what is going on in oneself. Socrates said *gnothi seauton* (know thyself!), and we are still learning what that means. We must know the taxonomy of our own paradigm, what our parents, culture and religion have taught us. We must know the shape and function of our individual

107

and collective paradigm so that we may know its grammar. And to know its grammar is to know what it allows and what it disallows; what are its blind spots, the points of terror that cannot be known, and what are its lacunae, the defects of any culture, language and religion. For instance, in Hindi, there is no verb for thanksgiving, which made it very difficult for the Jesuit missionaries who went out in the sixteenth century to teach the Indians about Christ and the central point in Christian prayer, the Eucharist, a thanksgiving. In China, there is really only a very loose concept of the divinity. Speaking of the Lord of Heaven there doesn't mean what we Christians, Jews and Muslims mean when we say it.

Naming demands that we know what we are about. In writing the novel we are allowing our own creations to dominate us so that we will be changed sufficiently to get on with more creation. They create us. This is the power of one's creation over the writer. It is also the power of all imaginative literature. The writer invents reality, and then it returns the compliment, a fact that modern literary criticism and its offshoot, biblical criticism, forget in their rush to reduce or deconstruct the invented myth to a non-truth forget. Any literature which symbols us and the real -- as opposed to bad literature which merely signs the real, thus glancing off it in an arbitrary way -- is true, and when it is sacred literature it becomes empirically true, true in our minds and hearts, true in our bodies, true in our histories. [As an aside, Nagarjuna was the father of Buddhist deconstructionism. For him, literature didn't work. It was pregnant with Emptiness [shunyata]. But that is his faith. And his writings bespoke, not a western-type deconstructionism or nihilism, but a positive spirituality of Emptiness. Literature works for us, all literature, and we believe in it all, not just in Holy Writ. Verification means nothing where this type of truth is concerned. When one has experienced such a truth it is as empirical as anyone wants.]

It would be well to rehearse Karl Rahner's epistemology here. This should not only illuminate my thoughts on method in seeing how giving oneself in sensibility to the sensibility of the other allows them to dominate us and tell us their names, but also it can well serve as a possible opening for dialogue with classical Buddhists such as Nagarjuna, Bhavaviveka and contemporary ones such as D.T. Suzuki and Keiji Nishitani and the rest of the Kyoto school. For Rahner, knowing is the being-present-to-the-self of being. As such, cognition and being are mutually constitutive. So, the knower's proper object is the self. So how does all this relate to naming and becoming dominated by the text, rite, etc. that one is trying to understand? In this way. For Rahner, abstraction has three moments. In the first, one is at one with the other in sensibility at the same time that one is present to oneself. This means that one allows the other [the intelligible subject in one's object] to dominate one so much that one becomes the other. For Rahner, sensibility means that the object becomes self-realized in an intuition. But to become an intuition the knower must become passive before the being of the other giving himself to the materiality of that other in empirical knowledge. The other impinges itself on one in such a way that the knowable element in matter [its *species intelligibilis*] takes hold of our physical faculties in so intense a way that they lose their identity in the known. The tryst of knowing is a carnal knowledge of the other in its very materiality. Thus, one becomes a text. One becomes a sky. One becomes Jesus, Yahweh, Allah, Buddha, a fly or turtle. The knower does not empty himself in the other in the ecstasis of knowing; rather, ecstasis happens *ex abrupto* to the knower causing a physical identity between him and the known. But human knowledge is more than this nature mysticism of cognitive identity with one's object. It is a process of nooifying matter, lifting it from its primal emptiness and removing it from its infinite capacity to be anything it wants by abstracting from it its specifying form, that which makes it what it is. Thus, the second moment is abstraction, in which the knower reclaims himself in withdrawing the *species intelligibilis* from the capacious yawn of matter and bringing it home to spirit thus transubstantiating matter into a spiritual self. If the first moment was spirit becoming dominated and transubstantiated into matter in sensibility's genuflection before prime matter, then the second moment reverses the process and matter becomes dominated by spirit in becoming spiritual in *species intelligibilis*. Thus, mystical, intuitional ecstasis reverses itself becoming the abstractional enstasis which we call a phantasm of the object. One's agent intellect flashes the particularity of this phantasm before the paradigmatic screens of its a priori, its prejudiced horizon, and a universal, a name, is born from a particular experience. "This is chalk", one says. From one point of view, one knows one's own knowledge, since all knowledge is knowledge of the knowing and known self. From another, the abstracted phantasm refers to that other, the known object. This allows Rahner to refute Kant's assertion that one cannot transcend space and time through knowledge. If the *Vorgriffe*, the preapprehension, is a capacity to know all being, then any being in the very process of being known refers back onto space and time, but also inward to the infinite which is the horizon of one's knowing. Thus, it is possible to know God as well as an apple, since there is a unity in all knowledge, a unity bespoken by the *Vorgriffe*. However, the infinite is not to be known in the object, but only indirectly in one's own inner horizon. The physical object is, thus, only at best a metaphor of the intentionality of that horizon. One is tempted to say the

109

'content' of that horizon; but that would be to make God an effect, a creature, and deprive him of his nature as not a part of what he created.

The third moment of abstraction and human knowing is the conversion of the intellect to the phantasm. In this moment Aquinas,and Rahner who retrieved him, sees a unity between sensible and intellectual knowledge. Only through the production of sensibility can the intellect realize its own essence. It creates sensibility as a power subordinate to it so that it might turn outward to the other where the agent intellect renders the phantasm intelligible by informing it with its a priori principles, the paradigms of the spirit itself.

But what does one know in knowing the world? One knows the metaphysical stuff of one's own intellect which has gone out and brought back the real of the world for it to know in judging it against the screen of its a prioris. This knowledge varies infinitely and hence is not univocal. It is analogical. (1)

It is well to note that the great analogy of the world is a human person. In this sense Jesus Christ is a metaphor of God, an analogy so domesticated by living and dying among us that he becomes analogy. He is like us as God, and is us as a man. He is unlike us as God, but is still one of us as man. God cannot speak univocally to us, it would kill us to communicate without the buffer of a human or mundane medium. The oblique is, thus, the language of the sacred: namely, in human form it is word and gesture and its elements that indirectly [that is, through their symbolic nature] initiate or originate the divine irruption; and, when this 'word' becomes scripture it is the coinage of the institutionalized religious analogy; always revealing, always hiding the revealed; always coming close, ever star-distant. The religious gestures eddy out and incorporate all the things and aspects of our lives: namely, water, oil, bread, relationships, etc. Hence, all our knowledge of God and the sacred is analogical, mediated through the *chiaroscuro* of symbol, of sacrament.

God gave himself to matter as the human spirit does in knowing the world. And in divinizing the *species intelligibilis* of our bodies, i.e. our souls, he becomes us in the knowledge we call grace, his self-donation in love. He appropriates us in knowing himself in us. He empties himself in matter only to transubstantiate that matter in the abstraction of divinizing grace, taking us into himself as one of his 'intellectualized' family. And then he takes himself back without going back on his incarnational ecstasis. God became matter in the analogy of

Jesus. We become God in the analogy of divinizing grace. In method as in spirituality one must give oneself to the very materiality of the symbol. One must lose oneself in text, rite, etc. to be found by the subject within it; to become it, so that, in the carnal knowledge of phantasm one's spirit might touch on the matter of the symbol and thus be named, baptized in the kenosis of losing oneself and being found and named by the other who imposes his name in our most interior recesses.

To return to method per se. The form of domination I outlined above was one in which one went out to the object to find the intelligible, the person within it. There is another form of domination, however; one in which one goes into one's own mind as into *terra incognita*. It all has to do with symbols as images. The symbol really points to something. When the young theologian sits down to exegete a text -- and exegesis is hermeneutics -- or to understand the dynamics of a religion he must allow the phenomenon to dominate him in the way something greater dominates us. We must have awe before it. It must be other than us. We are not creating an alter ego here. That would be eisegesis. The other must create us as the character creates himself in the novel. In this sense, the theologian is the amanuensis of the theological muse as Rimbaud was of the poetic muse. He becomes a seer, a shaman of a sort. Domination of the sort I am advocating is what Ignatian mysticism calls a *compositio loci*, a composition of place in which one goes -- for instance in the infancy narratives of the New Testament -- into the scene in Bethlehem where Jesus was born to smell the hay and manure, to touch the animals, pick up the child, talk with him and the Virgin, console Joseph in his troubles at the same time as one congratulates him. If the domination outlined in the Rahnerian mold is of the epistemological variety and performed by the agent intellect, this kind is the supreme act of the active imagination. Jungian psychology is good at this. Jung lectured for two years, from 1939-41, on the active imagination and the Spiritual Exercises of St. Ignatius of Loyola, the founder of the Jesuits. Today, the Jungian psychologist Ira Progoff (2) holds workshops teaching his clients to use the active imagination to draw up images from their unconscious and to dialogue with them. This technique of what he calls 'twilight imagery' is quite simple to master. One merely closes the eyes almost totally so that one won't be distracted by sight, keeping them open just enough that sleep doesn't overtake one. Then, being totally open to the topic under consideration, one waits for quietness and images to arise. It is surprising how quickly they do arise. When one has enough of them, one stops, writes them down and then begins to talk with them. More suprising is that they begin to take on a life of their own. They talk back with a freedom that makes one believe that one is inhabited by more then oneself. Progoff even offers to teach one how to set up a journal and dialogue with the parts of one's life. In theological methodology, this journal could be useful in structuring the imaging one is doing in order to 'get into' the other religion, or better, letting it come into oneself. The imagination, therefore, is a key to my thoughts on method. Freud said that the dream was the royal road to the subconscious. For our purposes, the subconscious is the storehouse of the a priori considered psychologically as the imagination. The way to the secular and religious a priori is through the image, whether one is asleep or awake. The theologian Morton Kelsey has done good work from a Jungian perspective on dream and its use in one's spiritual life. When Freud gave therapy to his patients, who were obviously awake, he let them talk in any way they wanted, in stream of consciousness, ultimately, when they began to trust him. Then all the contents of the unconscious began to pour out, frequently in images. Then he was getting somewhere. The thing was that he had to translate them for the patient since he had hidden their meaning from himself; he had forgotten that he had forgotten; remember Laing's formula for that? Repressed material demands to be imaged and then translated. The overwhelming majority of what one knows never comes to consciousness unless there is a psychological crisis in one's life and then all the content pours our autonomously, if one is psychotic, or just odd facets appear and dominate, if one is neurotic. (3) What I am advocating is that one allow the images to come, to talk with one freely. This not only demands work, it demands that one become quite exhausted, as one does when writing -- courting the images does a real number on one's body. In a word, I am asking that one give oneself to an inner power, the inner person that we are and don't know. For Freud it meant that one would go a bit bonkers since he was infecting his patient with his own neurotic bacillus by allowing the images of his illness to emerge so that he could, as St. Ignatius said, "relish the self", get a good dose of your own reality firsthand, in the mouth; taste it, roll it around and savor its essence. The monk Charles De Foucault used to teach those to whom he gave spiritual direction to say the prayer the Our Father, but with a twist. To show them just how much trust they really had in God the Dominant Father, he had them say the prayer to their husband or wife or best friend or religious superior. The results were shocking. It was a *compositio loci*. Putting them actually in the position of being engaged with someone real, someone they knew intimately, and then giving oneself to their will ['...Thy will be done..] was frightening. It opened them up to who they really were. Images appeared. Words offered themselves to express those images. A new mask appeared and a new name with it. The person was different from what he thought he was. It demanded courage and humility, docility, in a word, in the real meaning of that latinism: teachable. To be taught one has to sit at the master's feet. The theologian and historian of religions must delve ever deeper into himself to learn this docility before the images his own mind presents him not only about the object of his study, but about himself over against the external real of his study.

Thus, this is what I mean by allowing one to be dominated by the thing one is studying, trying to name it. It must name itself. One mustn't force it; one mustn't dominate it, it must dominate one, take control so that it can reveal itself, so that it can be other, be free to be itself; free to move around and speak; free to say things that we wouldn't say; free to shock; free to delight; free to challenge our darkness; free to be outrageous; free to be immoral; free to be moral; free to be man or woman, or both at the same time; free to be God. Here it would be worthwhile to mention Kenneth Burke's card trick. In his classic work *A Grammar of Motives* (4), Burke makes mention of a card trick that illustrates a point central to this essay. What the trickster wants is that the person in the audience choose exactly the card that he, the trickster, has forechosen for him, the Jack of Hearts. He chooses someone from the audience and then says to him,"Name four suits." The one chosen to help says, "Clubs, diamonds, hearts and spades." Then the leader says, "Choose two of them." If he says hearts and spades, the leader says choose one. If he says clubs and diamonds, thus leaving out the Jack of Hearts, the leader says, "Then that leaves hearts and spades. Now choose one of them." If the one chosen says spades, the leader says, "That leaves hearts. Now, name the four high cards in that suit." The one chosen says, "Ace, king, queen and jack." The trickster then says, "Choose two." If the chooser says ace and king, the trickster says, "That leaves queen and jack. Now choose one." Whatever the chooser says is correct: if he says the Queen of Hearts, the trickster says, "That leaves the Jack of Hearts." If the chooser says "Jack of Hearts", all the better. My point here is that when one has a paradigm and chooses according to it, it shapes the answer, not allowing the text, rite or any religious phenomenon to be other, to be itself. One imposes one's own meaning on it, one according to one's lights and darknesses. It is psychologically axiomatic that we don't see what we are looking *at*, we see what we are looking *for*. This is why Husserl and Freud tried to be suppositionless with their epoche and therapeutic method, respectively: they wanted the other to be himself. But where they failed was in their psychology. The mind can't withdraw and still be mind. It becomes so impoverished that it can't function, it cannot really see the other because it isn't working according to its nature. And the nature of the mind is to know the object as other.

113

Freud and Husserl impoverished reality too much in plying their method. Both the agent intellect and one's imagination must be in gear to find the name that one's object is trying to communicate to us. What I am advocating is that one use one's psychology and ontology of knowing (one's a priori) in order to let the other go beyond one's a priori and its paradigms to inform it -- I use 'inform in the Aristotelian sense of giving off its intelligibility -- with itself, in order that it tell the knowing subject what its own subjectivity is. Again, Marx was correct. The question shapes the answer. One must watch the questions one asks of the text or of any religious phenomenon. One's first obligation is to find what questions the religion asks. This means one's first obligation as religious scholar or scholar of religions is to listen, to place oneself at the other's disposal to take us where he will. This is difficult enough in studying another religion, but in trying to be docile to one's own, one must allow one's epistemological framework and one's active imagination to speak to one as if for the first time. One must see both the other's and one's own religion as if for the first time.

This involves the art and gift of listening. It creates an anxiety which is salutary. Ernest Becker says that there are two forms of anxiety: creative and destructive. The destructive types are those which dominate us because we lack the courage to go inside and name them. To name empowers us in our impotence before a force greater than ourselves. Naming makes our anxiety creative, a poesis -- a manufacturing process -- rather than something destructive. Fear of the scriptural text, of the church's power over one or over one's forebears; fear and its brother anger drive us to manhandle the text, reducing it to origins or functions, lessening it, driving the transcendent from us by sending false images and tangential intelligibilities to our imagination and intellect, respectively. Naming renders the text or phenomenon somewhat amiable. It creates an equality that allows the phenomenon freedom to move in one's imagination evoking further images and later concepts to emerge; and out of the images or thoughts emerge a name, not easily, but inexorably. Imaginative literature or imaginative architecture, creedal formulae, religious phenomena in general are products of the creative religious imagination. One approaches it only with the same faculty in oneself. Going into the text, rite or creed allowing one's creative imagination the freedom to do what it will bespeaks a faith in the goodness and health within us. There will be images too hard to handle, but it isn't necessary to be overwhelmed by them. When they are so powerful they reveal our own lacunae, the questions we refuse to ask, the questions our religion or culture forces us not to ask so that we can play the game of happy family. The Scriptures and creedal formulae force so many images of this sort that they become a criticism in reverse. Just as we have imposed the necessary force of our biblical and creedal criticism on them they reverse the process in becoming what they are: religious symbols instinct with the person who instituted or wrote them, be that God, prophet or saint. It's a poor game two can't play. Criticism is a two way street, we have had it all our way in the universities. Now *mythos* is beginning to have its day. The fundamentalists are only the antic fringe of those whose rationalism demands that the text be true in the way that their own paradigms command. They fear to let their imaginations loose, not their minds. Their minds are in gear, albeit low and going up a steep hill. But they are rationalists, not the irrational louts that we think they are. I am advocating, therefore, the irrationalism of the imagination as the first step to understanding our own or any other religion. Religion is always other, even if it is an other residing inside us as our own religion. It is always alien until we allow ourselves to be dominated by it as a transcendent meant to be served first -- submitted to in Islam and feared in the Judeo-Christian tradition -- and then befriended. The friendship comes from the transcendent since it is greater than we are, but it can only happen because we have allowed ourselves the openness, the obediential capacity, to be dominated by the real, and find it not dominating, but congenial, amiable. Thus, the name comes from within the phenomenon when we allow it into our a priori as active, creative imagination and matter giving up its secrets in the process of abstraction.

Criticizing our paradigm by finding out what its rules are so that we can find the *chiaro* (light) and *oscuro* (blindspots) of our a priori gives us room to grow as we discern the workings of the mind, which sends images through these grammars of our minds, and the paradigms are many, not one; they are a web, a pattern; when we send the images that arise through our paradigms, we arrive at a word, a name. When we do this enough we begin to find the paradigms within the text even as we find the paradigms in our own minds conceived as texts. But we must be aware that such verbalizing of our images, such mask-making, is an impoverishment at the same time that it is the making of, in the sense of invention of, our truth and the truth of the phenomenon studied.

Thus, just as making masks -- deriving words or images to symbol our inner reality that wants communicating -- impoverishes reality by making concepts pass through one's paradigms, so does naming impoverish the thing we conceive about what we are studying. Naming, therefore, isn't as easy as it looks. One must see what is in the phenomenon; see the thing, define its context, set up its relationship with the other phenomena in its field, then see its hidden frame, the hidden assumptions of its a priori as well as the hidden but operative questions it cannot and will not ask, its lacunae. If the questions we ask shape answers we arrive at, then the thing is to be willing to let the questions the other religion or our own asks shape us. The toughest hidden questions, however will be those of our own religion since we are so close to it. The most obvious thing in the Infancy Narratives of the New Testament is that the Magi story is a tale, but that came as a searing revelation to us in our own generation.

Naming demands that we listen to ourselves, to the ancillary and foundational disciplines of theology and religious studies, such as philosophy -- since the common base for both philosophy and theology is metaphysics -- and the empirical sciences, so that we know the best thinking the so-called secular world can bring to us. Bernard Lonergan went out and learned mathematics, physics and was doing a major work on economics at the time of his death. He could speak as authoritatively on Eskimo soapstone carvings and hockey as on philosophy and theology. One does not have to be a polymath to be a theologian, but one must know the general outlines, at least, of what our contemporaries are thinking. Vision, to be vision, must be in touch with the surfaces of the real. That is all that it can do. That is all that phenomenology can do. The theological moment arrives when we wish to go beyond what we see on the surface to find what is underneath. This is not yet the moment of meaning, the hermeneutical moment. It is still the moment of seeing , the surface and the infrastructure of the reality we would like to have in tow. But we will never have it 'in tow'. Hinduism knows that. All one can have is an *upanishad*, a near approach to truth, kneeling down before it. Aquinas and Aristotle before him knew that the surd of the intelligible was unintelligible matter. While I'm on the subject of surds, just a word on evil as a theological category. Evil has been 'out' and 'fragility' in, in order to break away from bad preaching that froze us all in our guilt. But evil is a reality, not just a privative thing as Augustine would have it. Emil Fackenheim, the Hegelian philosopher and master of Jewish thought, said that anyone who had gone through the Holocaust -- as he had -- knew that evil was real, palpable. He is somewhat an embarrassment to his young Jewish colleagues in Toronto, many of whom would rather get on with things and leave the past to the past. But Lonergan had something to say that I find helpful. He said that even God doesn't understand evil. The mysteries of the faith have an excess of intelligibility, we can never exhaust it. But sin and evil depart from rationality in God's and our mind. And what is irrational cannot be understood, forgiven, maybe, but not understood. Hence sin has a radical defect in intelligibility making it an absolute objective falsity, as Aquinas

116

would put it. But the modern paradigm doesn't like sin or evil. This is both a blind spot and lacuna in our thinking. We don't like to ask that question. It is as embarrassing to a theologian as the topic God is in polite company. I remember posing the question, Do you believe in the devil? to my colleagues from Hinduism, Buddhism and Islam. To a person, they said that they did. And one well-known scholar said that he had been exorcised as a child in India. It would be difficult to understand the other religions without seeing that sin and evil are hidden in our own paradigm and frame (mask) as questions we don't like to ask. Not asking it, not seeing it in the other religion as well as our own, is to miss something possibly essential. Certainly, without sin Christ would be otiose, a silly religious phenomenon dancing a pavan with the devil on the way to the cross.

Thus, the moment of naming does not employ epoche for all the reasons given above. My secular and religious a prioris (my two faiths), fuse in the religious existential in the transcendental unity that we call knowledge. Religious faith brings the secular faith [openness to the goodness of things] to abruptly discontinuous heights by the divinity's ability to compose reality in ways we desire, but couldn't hope for. Excluding both faiths, which is what epoche demands, would eviscerate the feeling-knowing capacity of my mind and heart. Thus, to 'see' at all it becomes necessary to compose reality as secular and religious by turns, at times; at other times, I see them as coterminous; these latter moments are graced in Christianity.

When you name the thing and then step back to see its relationships, its patterns, it becomes necessary to apply to what one sees the art of the historian, if one is doing the history of religions, or that of the theologian if one is pursuing that discipline in one's own or another religion. The series of patterns demand a deeper meaning, one this third moment, that of seeing, pattering, and naming cannot give.

II
The Fourth Moment:
Hermeneutic

It is now necessary to begin the fourth moment, that of stepping back and asking 'Quid significat?' -- what does all this mean? The historian moves through the text and artifacts of religion to find a person there, a man or woman in immediate contact with God or the self or its surrogate, as is the case with Nagarjuna and the Buddhist anthropology

117

holding that there is no self [anatta]. This is the moment of the seer when historian becomes artist, when *logos* becomes *mythos*; i.e. when things are writ larger than life because they are so, in reality. Meaning comes on two levels: *logos* gives us the knowledge of religious facticity. *Mythos* gives us the wisdom factor, allowing us to see it with transcendental eyes, perceiving somewhat intuitively the One, the True and the Good in the thing or person studied. The phenomenon becomes, ultimately, epiphany in the history of religions. It can never be a secular study since its object is not an object at all, but a religious subject. This is the moment when heart speaks unto heart in the sense that the felt-known symbolized becomes known by the scholar. The mask of Christ or of any religion reveals itself as *oscuro* in the secular darknesses to which we fall prey, and a luminous *chiaro* in the experience of the Ultimate.

The historian assigns meaning as seer, as an artist on the deepest level of his own a priori, the very ontological capacity to know (shaped by all the influences of his life and heritage) brought to bear on another's religion. The bits and pieces become a whole much greater than the parts. They become an intuition made because they are intelligible and demand to be known. But not everyone can know them. A truly secular person can know Buddhism up to and including its secular faith in the goodness of *samsara* (an endless and painful skein of lives). But unless one has had a faith that opens one to the discontinuous transcendentalityof religious faith, one cannot do the history of religions. Religious faith adds a dimension of immediacy to the Truth that pure secularity can only hint at. All disciplines are faiths of a secular sort: a belief that they will yield results and therefore throw one's subject open to view. But the secular a priori and its active phase as paradigm in action can go only so far. It can know the transcendentals as hopes, not as being possessed by them. The religious person who is historian can go much further. He can go from his Truth to the Truth of Buddhism or Judaism, etc. And this is not because he is better; he isn't. But he is different, qualitatively. The religious existential in Christianity, the divinized secular a priori, has given us a new heart and mind. The religious person can be seer as no purely secular person can be. He can see into the heart and know the mind. He can intuit *mythos* and know *logos* and know where they belong and leave them intact both in and after his hermeneutical musings are over.

The historian of religions doesn't work from revealed data as does the theologian of religions, but his secularly trained mind is transmuted by the divinized existential of religious faith. As such, it is faith which makes the religious historian of religions capable of understanding another religion more fully than his non-religious colleague because in faith one puts on the mind and heart of the transcendent. In Christianity it is the mind and heart, the whole feeling and thinking apparatus, which is slowly transubstantiated into that of the deity. The divinizing existential presence of Christ and the Holy Spirit are efficacious here. In Buddhism, it is the individual's own transcendence which transubstantiates him into his own Buddhanature. Religion changes people; that is its purpose. There is an intrinsic change which takes place in Christianity because of the efficacious presence of Christ in one's secular unconditionality and autonomy which makes them a human-divinized unconditionality and autonomy. One becomes infinitely greater in these two facets of one's a priori, but one holds on to them with supernal lightness, which means with love. One knows as if one is not knowing, loves as if one is not loving -- without clutching. The historian who is religious in this sense can know much, much more of the other religion than one who merely understands his secular a priori.

The theologian of religions goes beyond the facticity of the religion in question in a way that the historian cannot. He can do this since he works from revealed sources on the data presented by the other religious person. One's personal experience may be paradigmatic for his finding his own divinized a priori -- the locus of the Self and of God --, but it is not normative for the Church. The experience of the church is normative, but not necessarily paradigmatic. Paradigm in this sense is a way of learning God, of finding him again and again in the same place, of thinking and reaching conclusions. A church norm is a gathering of the experiences of the Revelation into a metaparadigm able to fit individual paradigms -- i.e. resonate with them, enliven them, to tell them they are alright with God or not -- ; able to guide the individual and collective experiences of God in the lives of its communicants and challenge both in order to vector them back on the Revelation of God and the God of Revelation. As such, a norm -- dogma -- is larger , though not necessarily richer, than a paradigm. Dogma is the *mythos* for the church; paradigm is the *mythos* for the individual, extruded from his own story.

The theologian of religions, therefore, works from both his individual *mythos* and that of his church and brings them to bear on the religions in question. He uses the craft of the historian, the phenomenological tools and the artist's charism as seer to view the religion and draw forth a hermeneutics with which both he and the

119

adherents of the other religions will be comfortable. But he goes further than the historian since his data trove contains revelation not just as background *Gestalt*, but as his most proximate tools. The paradigms he has learned in his own life become his individual masks; he has found God in his life and learning time and again through the experience of articulating his self and God in what becomes his mask of truth. But the metamask of norm is the collective mask of revelation and dogma, both of which derive from the church, the one under the Holy Spirit's inspiration to write, the other under its guidance to teach. The individual paradigm sends him out to the other religious person armed with the way he found God in his own life time and again. This allows the individual religious heart to speak unto the individual religious heart. But the church's mask as norm sends him back to the Scriptures and magisterial statements so that these may sustain his personal inadequacies and enlighten their dark places; i.e. throw light where he has not been graced but where the church as a whole has been. The theologian has much more at his disposal than the historian, therefore. The latter is a religious person going it alone, using his divinized existential as the grammar (paradigm) to unlock the mysteries of the other religion. The theologian is enlightened by the wisdom of the Scriptures and by the masks of truth, the symbols of his faith which have sustained Christians for centuries. The theologian as seer is never alone. He works alone, but he is also a we. This is why the church is so interested in its theologians: they represent their brothers and sisters. They never say anything just on their own even as they must say it alone; i.e. they must go out on the ice by themselves in order to discover new truths for us.

Precisely, therefore, how do we arrive at patterns in the religious phenomenon? The psychologists help us here. First we must look to the historical successes or failures of the religion as a family in order to see the patterns there. These successes and failures tend to repeat. They show us the illuminating points (*chiaro*) and the blindspots (*oscuro*) of the religion by showing us the questions it asks and those it refuses to ask. Second, check the ritual or liturgy of the religion. Memory is embedded in rite. In Catholicism there is an axiom that is helpful here: *lex orandi, lex credendi*, the church prays according to its beliefs. Belief is the memory of the church acted out in rite so as to catechize as it evokes the presence of the deity. Third, see what happy family games the text or religious phenomenon manifests. This is another way of getting at the lacunae of the religion, the spots of pain and repression forcing questions or possibilities away from the group to keep it intact. Fifth, is there any Group Think manifested here? Is there any authority principle acting invisibly as a frame or visibly demanding belief? Lastly, as the

120

relationships gather into something cohesive, into a web of meaningful rules or paradigms, which of the paradigms is paramount? In the Gospel of Mark, which paradigm shapes the redactor-writer's mentality, shaping what material he will include and telling him what theological points to make? The mask or symbol is a face of related tissues. Anatomists define a bodily organ as a gathering of tissues to perform a function. The mask or symbol is just that: a gathering of disparate elements joined by its own inner truth. As symbol it is the culmination of the desire and necessity of the writer or artist of any sort to communicate himself within his religious truth and his truth within himself. As he does it he disappears. His art remains, his personality remains, but it is changed into art, into words or the lines of a statue or monument. He has given himself to us to study, to know. Patterns emerge as names attract because of the laws of attraction and repulsion imposed by grammars. We know when things ring correctly. Or, at least, someone wise and learned among us knows when things are put together according to hoyle. The theologian must look for that hoyle in the part and the rest of its *Gestalt*. A flaw in today's naming and patterning methodologies is that they become so powerful that we forget what we are about. We forget that there is a religion here, a *mythos* which can never be dominated by *logos*. *Logos* serves *mythos*. When we forget this, we end up misconstruing it, giving signs instead of symbols to our readers. And when the signs are brilliant, they are all the more dangerous. Heresy is a truth too far, one pushed beyond its capacity to convey human meaning. But it is an attractive mistruth because it plugs into the truth of those it attracts, but in a way so arbitrary -- in a way so swayed by the fads and needs of the moment -- that it takes freedom away, the freedom to make *logos* shine on *mythos* to see if it *is* symbol or sign.

Thus, theology can be done only by a believer, one who has a living *mythos* within. And I question whether religious studies can be done without belief of some kind in the religious. The very adjective religious means that one has a relation with the deity. We don't speak of 'religion studies', do we? Thus, if one's secularity is instinct with that openness which bespeaks a trust in the goodness of things and people, that is a faith sufficient to be what Paul said is salvific: a healthy conscience followed.

My own faith has allowed me both as historian and theologian to see Nagarjuna's concept of the secular, *samsara*, as being much more than it would purport to be without the deepening and enriching power which religious faith affords. Because of my own Christian view of the radically human and secular as the arena of the holy and divine, I can and do perceive something more in *samsara* than an endless surd burdening us with its boredom and pain. The Buddhist secular is precisely that; it is not a secular one, it is a religious one. That changes it unalterably from one in which the best one's unconditionality and autonomy can hope for is an apprehension of the True, the Good and the Unity we all need. The axiom *nirvana* is *samsara* means that one is in immediate contact with transcendence and it is precisely because it is secular that it is *nirvana*, not in spite of it. Buddhism does not escape (*moksha* = a liberation from) the ultimately cloying grandeur of the world at its best, and pain at its worst; rather, Buddhism courts it since its faith is that at its core there is bliss. Thus, I do not see Buddhism as a quintessentially secular philosophy, but as a religion. Philosophy can only pose the question about the True, the Good and the One; it can only pose the question about ignorance, evil and an eschatological entropy. But it can **do** nothing about it since philosophy is by definition a discipline which changes the mind, not the real. Religion, in posing the great questions about our aetiology and teleology, about what we term theodicy -- is God worth it? bringing God to the bar of human criticism -- does not stop there. It brings a solution to the problem of pain. All religion begins when we confront pain in a praxis way, not a theoria way. Theistic religions have God coming down to us and doing something for us and telling us how to be religious by being human; telling us how to worship and find fulfillment. A non-theistic religion like Buddhism and Advaitan Hinduism, have us doing it ourselves. We become the source of our own revelation, that is why there were to be no Sutras as such in Buddhism; the secular is an hierophany and that is enough to bring about the luminous experience of *nirvana* releasing us to be human fully at the same time that we become fully religious; and in both Christianity and Buddhism both are coterminous and happen simultaneously.

Buddhism, therefore, is not a natural religion. There is no such thing. That doesn't make it supernatural either for the reasons given above: the supernatural as category does not compute at all in Nagarjuna's Buddhism and it has become shopworn and a bit illegitimate in Christianity. Buddhism is a religion; it is the quintessential religion of the human, of human unconditionality and autonomy. No heteronomous norm can guide us all. Since the Buddha is unique in each, then total deconstruction is necessary intellectually and emotionally in order to allow the faith in this truth to recompose one in one's secularity in a way that allows one to live fully human in this fully secular world. As theologian aided by the dogmas and revelations of my own faith, I find it easy to understand Buddhism in this way. Buddhism says that one is unconditioned but not infinite. Christianity says that one is divinized and unconditioned, but not infinite. The Christian heart-mind (the felt-known of my a priori) is, then, the royal road to Buddhism for me. (9) There can be no other. As my own story finds God in my life, constantly changing his name as he reveals himself ever more deeply and richly, my paradigmatic changes (growth in wisdom and love altering my a priori) demand that and cause my inauthentic, temporary, masks, not to be ripped away as they were with Freud and Marx, but in their flawed secularity to become purified and be the medium (as *oscuro*, the surd of our darknesses and sins) of the *chiaro*. And slowly, painfully, joyfully, peacefully, my mask becomes my truth so that, finally God is to be found only in those most painful masks which hide my nakedness. Masks must hide the holy since it is subject and impatient of full revelation, even to oneself. But they must also reveal both the holy God and the holy self to the self and others. This is why I accepted Rahner's concept that the symbol, one's a priori articulated in paradigm and masked as symbol (as imagined by the faith), is primarily for the self and only secondarily for others. Masks are the best we can do. They are our truths, both in the Madhyamika of Nagarjuna's Buddhism and in Christianity. They are different masks, but there is much that is humanly understandable and analogous in both.

Masks are devices for distancing oneself from one's inner truth; both the good and evil of that truth are too much to take directly and all at once. Masks parcel out that truth in symbolic particles the easier to handle. As such, masks play a necessary role. For, if we are truly made in God's image then full immediacy -- the mystical union with the self -- would kill us because that awful epiphany is too unbearable, not because of the evil it contains but because of the dilation it causes the heart because of our good. The saints cried out to God for no more of it because that kind of love was too powerful for their poor hearts. We fear to see the self *qua* self because we think it an apocalypse of evil and, as such, would kill us. But evil won't kill, just atrophy. Good kills because one isn't prepared for the full force of its loving insistence, the thrust to be everywhere caressing the most obscure folds of our inner recesses. If to see God is to die, then to see ourselves is too. Masks of truth are salvific because they distance us from the death force of truth, which force is the good. We take it in dribs and drabs and hate ourselves for our mediocrity, crying for full manifestation and complete union with the self, when all we can really handle is the elusive glimpse of that sly being afforded by reason, theology, art and the asymptotic sacramental brushes given by religion. Masks are the necessary sacraments holding our fullness even as they hide it, as God is held and obscured by the kind old sacramental signs the church finds salvific.

The secular a priori can empower one with an hermeneutics of suspicion, searching out the inauthentic, the inhuman in religion and ourselves. The religious a priori, fused with the criticism of the secular a priori, can come to Ricoeur's second naivete, which is an hermeneutics of innocence, one of faith in which one is ever open to the blind spots and lacunae in one's secular and religious self and that of the religion under scrutiny. Thus there is a critical polarity here: one plies between the meaning of oneself and the self one finds in the text, rite or creed one is studying. One's own suspicion checks oneself as one is over against the object of scrutiny. One finds out who he is in relation to others. The reverse is also true, the other reveals itself as it challenges our own hidden assumptions, the questions we, our culture and religion are afraid to ask. Meaning comes from insight borne of changing the reality one views in the viewing, and that reality is both inner and outer. Meaning is a confluence, therefore, of the truth of the self found in past experiences and the present experience of finding the self in the other person as text, rite, etc. Meaning is only human meaning, there is no other. There can be no other hermeneutic but a human one, a personalistic one. Any device, any criticism which cuts away at the human *mythos* and logos -- be it literary or theological methodology -- damages both the self and the self one wishes to find in the religion in question. Our a priori knowledge and judgments meet the self within and without to form a posteriori judgments. When Kant turned us to the transcendent self within he did well. When empiricism turned us to the object since it couldn't get a handle on the inner self and replicate its findings under laboratory conditions, it did us damage. Hermeneutics is, therefore, a dance between a transcendental method and an empirical one: the first one looking for the unarticulated presences, ours and God's, within in order to limn out an ontology of knowing and a philosophical-theological anthropology; the second, empirical, method being bound by the facticity of things and the rules of logic. Logic is the explicit method brought to the implicit method run by our a prioris, both secular and religious. Both are necessary logics, though. To scotch out the transcendental logic is to scotch out the logic of the transcendent itself. And to eschew the empirical is to confound the incarnational aspect of truth, its finitude and its materiality.

III

Method as Grid

I have outlined the ways the mind works and the shapes it takes as it goes out to know people and things. The method of the a priori is an implicit one, working behind the scenes. I have outlined how to raise it to view so that one may see it, evaluate it, criticize it and reshape it, if necessary, so that it may be more useful in knowing the truths of religion. On the awareness level, one learns and chooses from a variety of methodologies in religious studies and theology. In Biblical studies we have learned how to isolate the bits and pieces of the book by employing the tool of literary forms in order to get at the author's intent and the book's meaning. We have learned to get back to the community and the editor-author of the individual gospels by using redaction criticism. This opened up the community in which and for which the gospel was written. We have learned to use Levi-Strauss' structuralism in order to further divine the dynamics of meaning included in our sacred books. And, with Baruch Halpern in his *The First Historians: The Hebrew Bible and History* [San Francisco: Harper & Row, 1988] we have learned, once again, to take our biblical history as not only the nirvana of *Heilsgeschichte* but as the mundane samsara of secular history. We have come full circle to a naivete of faith, but not without the interstate highways our methodologies provided us with. All these methods are the tools of the secular literary critic. In this sense, a book and The Book are the same: they reveal themselves to the critic. This essay is not a 'how to' in the sense of teaching you these methods. You can pick up any of a number of good monographs on them.

But, in all these explicit methods, it is well to remember my demonstration of the working of the word's generation through the agency of the interactions of the a priori, paradigm -- subject, in other words -- and object. As the subject generates the word, that very mask becomes less capable of taking in all that is going on in the object. Cognition and word formation, therefore, impoverish the reality we wish to know. Reason is richer than the words it produces; and reality is richer and denser than any word can convey. I have emphasized the ontological, epistemological, linguistic and psychological aspects of method in order to elucidate them and buttress my thesis, that we must use our interiority in method if we wish to work effectively at our craft.

125

I have emphasized my own religious background, Roman Catholicism, to say two things: I find it necessary and useful in method, and to say that we Catholics, in general, do religious studies and theology differently from Protestants and secularists or any stripe. In theology, we have been outsiders peering back, not so much at our originating sources, but at ourselves, and that for centuries. In this country we lived in a most comfortable ghetto in order to keep our identities. Ask a Philadelphian where he comes from in 'Philly' and he will name you his parish, not his neighborhood or street. We have been outsiders here in the U.S. because our Protestant forebears both feared and despised us. The public schools we came to were Protestant parochial schools -- secularized, to be sure, but Protestant in ethics, culture and outlook. There has never been separation of church and religion here in America. And separation of church and state wasn't really emphasized until the 'Paddies', Germans and Jews began to come here in great numbers in the last century. We Catholics set up our own parochial schools to keep our identities as much as our faith. We are different. We wanted to think and feel differently, to maintain our old a prioris and yet still be Americans, so we set up schools and paid for them out of our own pockets. We were excluded and we, in turn, excluded. President Kennedy's father, Joseph, said that he went everywhere with the great men of Boston, everywhere, that is, but to their homes. An interesting joke came out of the election campaign between Nixon and Kennedy. A Boston Protestant went up to a neighbor and friend, and, pointing his finger accusingly said, "You voted for Kennedy because he's a Catholic." The Boston Irishman rejoined, "You got it wrong. I voted for Kennedy because *I'm* Catholic."

The Second World War brought the boys together for the first time. Men formed unbreakable bonds in the brotherhood of the foxhole. We changed. They changed. The GI Bill allowed many of 'our boys', to go to college who would never have had that chance. A new generation was aborning: Catholic intellectuals. Not just Catholic doctors and lawyers trained in Catholic universities. But Catholic intellectuals, a laity trained in the Harvards and Stanfords of the land. The Ecumenical Council opened up the same possibility for the clergy and nuns. They flocked to the great secular 'grad' schools both here and abroad. We drank deeply of the learning of the great men and women who were our mentors. I was one of that generation. But a gnawing doubt remained with me: Though I absorbed so much of the new knowledge and culture, changing me as Catholic and theologian, I still knew that I was different. I think and feel differently about things, the important things in my life, than do Protestants. The formative process in the graduate schools I studied in both here and abroad changed me. I learned many of the new and wonderful things about theology and religious studies that I didn't know when I did theology professionally just before the Council. But I kept wondering how I could be Catholic when I prayed and secular when I thought, especially when that secularism was really Protestant thinking. This book is the culmination of years of thinking, therefore. It is a cry of the heart, that we have things to learn from each other. It is a cry of the mind that we must use our interiority in order to know. The explicit grids we impose on our sacred things are shaped by our implicit paradigmatic grids. It is well to know them both. I hope this short essay aids in some small way in doing that.

IV

Concluding Thoughts

In this little primer on hermeneutical method, I have called for a change on the part of my brothers and sisters whose a prioris don't easily allow their interiority in general or the mystical dimension in religion, in particular, into the study of religion; be they Protestants, secularists, or agnostics, or Catholics who have not drunk deeply enough at their own well. A final word on masks in the light of the findings of cognitive psychology will summarize my thesis that there are different ways of being Christian and that they help or hinder us in 'doing' religion in an academic way.

The Scottish psychologist R.D. Laing says that all families have rules concerning family relations, about what may be put into words and with what words it may be expressed. This holds for religions, too. We cohere as groups -- even Buddhism, the most fey of religions -- calls for belief in the Community as one of its trinity of foundational dogmas. As groups, we live off vital truths. But, couldn't it be said that these same truths can be and often are turned into vital lies in the name of keeping the religious family going? I think so. This would be the negative side of the mask of religious truth I've written about in this essay. The vital lie appears when the revealed datum is taken over by the necessity of institutionalizing that truth. These vital lies are to be found in our a prioris. These are the assumed consensus on which the individual and group operate. When the truth becomes a vital lie it is to keep us whole and safe and religious by masking us from the possibility of knowing anything that will hurt us more than we can bear. As such, the game called 'happy family' by the cognitive psychologists tells us what we can know and what we cannot know. The controller would be the religious a priori, the core of the individual and the group alike. 'Group Think' constrains the information-seeking power of the brain in order to keep

127

the group's assumptions integral, to give it confidence and hope in times of trial. Creeds are not only genial masks formulating the truths of the group, but when the family tells one that the truth can only be said 'this way, and not that way', it keeps the brain from knowing on the awareness level what is happening on an unconscious level. This phenomenon the cognitive psychologists call 'blindsight'. It means that one part of the mind can know something while awareness is oblivious of it. Daniel Goleman's thesis is that "Much consequential mental activity goes on outside awareness." This is not a new truth. But the psychologists are coming up with clinically proved evidence that the brain shields individuals, and *a fortiori* groups, from knowing things on the upper level that it knows on a perceptual and even conceptual level unconsciously.

Thus the brain reads things unconsciously most of the time since most mental processes go on prior to awareness. The transfer of information from one part of the brain to the other is inhibited by the vital lie of repression. This keeps unwanted or upsetting information from coming to awareness. It is a faulty transfer of information. The semantic memory filters the relevant and irrelevant information through schemas which organize perception. I have called such schemas paradigms in this essay. These schema/paradigms interact constantly and with consummate delicacy with attention. They tell us what we can and cannot notice; i.e. they misdirect the mind even as they direct it. From the work of these active schema/paradigms we derive our information.

Applying this to the thoughts of this essay on the way Catholics and Protestants, for example, go about 'doing religion', I conclude that both communions have turned their prejudices into vital lies to keep from knowing certain aspects of the other which they deem harmful and upsetting to public order. We Catholics didn't allow ourselves to know how terribly Christian were Luther's intuitions about the necessity of faith in the process of salvation. We didn't like to think of the salvific power of Protestant baptism or about the fact that in Protestant orders that *ecclesia supplet* no matter what the communion. That the church supplies both the power and jurisdiction to a duly appointed minister because God wants the baptized to share his life celebrated liturgically, and that minister has 'valid orders'. This is so as a reflex principle even in the old Catholic theological manuals, the fine print after each theological theme [*tractatus*], where the living church keeps humanizing the lofty dogmas people have difficulty following.

Protestants didn't like the sound of bells and the sweet smell of incense. They bridled at the sight of monks and nuns, seeing them as otiose in the faith. Meditation and contemplation were out as theological categories and religious praxis. 'Spirituality' was not a subject taught in Protestant seminaries until most recently; it was a 'Catholic' conceit and discipline. This brings me to mysticism and mystical religions. One of the vital lies Protestants lived off, their game of 'happy family' which allowed them not to see upsetting truths, was that mysticism was not a central way to God, and it might even be an evil. Catholic thought begins from a good premise by preserving the finite human in all its goodness, flaws and evil. What is called Original Sin, what we would call the human condition today, did not destroy the *imago Dei* which causes our goodness. It vitiated it, though. But Catholic thought, in trying to emphasize the sacred in sacrament and priesthood, ended by overemphasizing the sacred, thus deprecating the very humanity it tried to preserve. It deprecates us by overloading us with the infinite. God is too much for us. Why did he come as a human? Because we could not abide him as he is. Didn't we learn that with Moses and that prophet's overload of God? This form of sacral overload ends in supernaturalism. And the logic of supernaturalism culminates with the heresy of the Manichee all over again. It is a fear of the human, of the bodily and finite dimensions. It wants to instill the divine and angelic in us so much that our humanity all but disappears. William F. Lynch in an essay in "Thought" (5), said that the three main cultural forms of the Manichee are a rebellion against the absurd that we find in human limits rendering one constantly scandalized by our humanity, unable to bear it, unable to forgive it, unable to like it. It demanded a Nietzsche to save us from this *ressentiment* (rage against our condition) by offering us a joy in the necessary offal of our nature, freeing us from such angelism and Puritanism to become ourselves. The second cultural form of the Manichee demands that the faith set up an elite and that the elite break away from the common herd in search of integrity, purity and freedom. The third cultural form of the Manichee is a flight from the body. At bottom, the Manichee is in rebellion against the finite. It is a heresy, not so much because it is an untruth badly stated, but because it is a truth too far and is supernally well stated. As an elitism, its exponents are brilliant, elegant and noble. Who could deny them? The church could and did. We are not an elitism. In this, Nietzsche was wrong. Despising the *hoi polloi*, he wanted no mediocrity around him and decried the plethora of mediocrities he found in the church. Calvinism, both in its European and North American manifestations, contained this angelic elitism. Catholics were looked down on as allowing less than the ideal; the Italian Church is always cited as the example, thus missing the humanity of that warmest and kindest of Christian people.

Protestantism began badly by deprecating humanity in raising grace to such high levels, but ended well by discovering a spirituality in human limits. Protestants found God in the streets, in commerce and human endeavor. It began in supernaturalism and ended in naturalism. What began with the rejection of any mediation of the finite between God and us ended with a sacramental system of the secular. To see only capitalism and the crude hubris of modernity as emanating from Protestantism's openness to the modern, is to malign it. It found God in the world, and one can't scant that.

The Protestant paradigm is weak on history, though. Catholic sacraments say that he is here, in that wafer, in that man kneeling to confess his sins, in that suffering marriage, in that cancer ward where oil finds grace in a lesion. The Protestant weakened the link between *mythos* -- the religious reality in human imaginative form -- and *kairos*, Greek for doing something at the opportune time. And isn't *kairos* the virtue of hope where God does something for us where we don't expect him? The Protestant emphasis on grace deemphasized the Christ as hierophany (manifestation of the sacred), and as kratophany (manifestation of power). Doing away with the evil of clericalism and triumphalism in the priesthood helped to atomize the presence of Christ among Protestants. But the New Testament says he takes up his home 'in us', not 'among us', as classical Protestant exegesis and ecclesiology had it. C.G. Jung said that when Protestants did this to the Scriptures they destroyed the *mythos* of the faith.

When the Protestant is healthy he finds God in the secular. When he is unhealthy he makes it all secular, as in the more muscular forms of the social gospel and in the misconstrual of Calvin on which capitalism as a spirituality is based; all of which Lynch would see as Pelagian, a rebellion, resentment, or the exaltation of the human conquering in pain. I would add that in the myth of Prometheus God hated us at our best, condemning us for our hubris. One can take the secular so far that one forgets that one is creature, not Creator; one forgets that we serve transcendence, not vice versa.

The other side of the coin in unhealthy Protestantism is to make the world all sacred, as in fundamentalism. Finding a hierophany in Tobias' dog wagging its tail in greeting its master is to make the tale wag the dog. When the Catholic is healthy he finds God in his limits: time, sin, place, play, etc. When he is unhealthy he flees these limits for *mythos* pure and simple, without the human dimension the Greeks found in their troika of *drama, pathos* and *mathos* -- human activity [drama] produces suffering [pathos], which, in turn, produces insight [mathos].

If the cognitive psychologists are correct, and evidence seems to be leaning heavily in their direction, then 'doing' religion demands that we know not only our vital truths, mask and a priori [their underside], but also *their* underside, our vital lies, front and underside. This means that Catholics will have to come to the realization that God lives as fully in Protestantism as in Catholicism, and vice versa. I have said that Catholic scholars have been seared by the vital lies of their a prioris just by going to the great Protestant and secular universities and having their assumptions challenged in such telling ways. The other side of the coin is that Protestant and secular scholars will have to articulate not only their vital truths, but their vital lies as well. To sing out *Credo in unum Deum* demands that we also sing out *credo in sanctam ecclesiam*. But, implicit in this final assertion is the necessity of being critical of the church in the assumptions which undergird the faith. The brain turns truth and the very ability to perceive it into masks of deception to keep us alive. That morbid necessity does not absolve us as theologians and historians of religions from being critics of our vital lies. This essay is about truth being our mask. I end with the hope that mutual criticism will reveal some of our vital lies, the masks of our morbidity so that we may exorcise them with vital truths. If Paul Ricoeur is correct, and I think he is, then it is precisely in these morbidities that we shall find our vital truths. Our darknesses refract all of us, our good and our evil, our originating affirmations as well as the inherited or willed fragilities that crush us. To avoid our darknesses, our blindspots, our masks, is to avoid the salvific truths lying pulsating within them. That takes courage, the kind Tillich called for; the kind Ernest Backer called for when he said that neurosis is rooted in word poverty [Revolution in Psychiatry], the inability to name and classify our experiences and go beyond the limits of our culture and childhood formation.

If my hypothesis and that of the psychologists is correct, the transcendent is radically different for all the religions, even within the same one, as it seems to be with Protestants and Catholics. This means that some religions are so rooted in culture and language that they interdict certain possibilities; that is to say, the deity or religious impulse which gives them life must take on the human forms it finds. This leads one to the possibility of the a priori being not only different among religions, it seems quite possible that it is different among different nationalities and racial groups. (6) This means that the way one 'does' religion or any discipline must be true to one's interiority. And that

131

demands that it will be different for people from different groupings religiously or culturally. I do not look for a homogenization of approaches down the line if, for instance, Protestants and Catholics become aware of their blunted sensibilities in some of the areas outlines above. One's link with the transcendent is different in the different religions and Christian communions; that alone ensures our individuality. What I hope for is not sameness, but fairness. This demands that one know oneself and be sufficiently challenged by the truth masks of others to change. It takes love and humility for the theologian and historian of religions to ply this route. But can we demand less?

A final caveat. Reality is too fugitive to admit of easy or lasting taxonomies. This is because we are the mystery trying to understand ourselves. That is what subjectivity entails and means. Any method must give way before the imperatives of a pushy, painful reality. Truth is a relationship, lasting, somewhat stable, but always on the move. Heraclitus lives. All is flux. But, truth is our mask.

Endnotes for Chapter VI:

Method, the Third and Fourth Moments

1. I am indebted to Prof. Jennifer Rike of Boston University for her insights into Rahner and Aquinas. These appeared in her doctoral thesis from the University of Chicago: *Being and Mystery: Analogy and Its Linguistic Implications in the Thought of Karl Rahner*. Chicago, 1986, pp. 161-201, passim. This will be published in different form by Harper & Row, San Francisco within the year. Aquinas' epistemology is taken from Rahner's *Spirit in the World*, pp. 95-97. Translated by William Dyche. New York: Herder and Herder, 1968. Her fusion of David Burrell's ideas on analogy with those of Rahner offer a major challenge to Protestant thinkers and Roman Catholics insufficiently aware of the *Ur* Aquinas doctrine of analogy. She, though Protestant herself, has retrieved the doctrine of the *analogia entis*, thus offering a language by which one may speak of God.

2. Ira Progoff has written prolifically about his method. To mention a few of his works that might prove beneficial to the methodologist, we might offer *Jung, Synchronicity, and Human Destiny: Non Causal Dimensions of Human Experience*. New York: the Julian Press, 1973. Then there is *Depth Psychology and Modern Man: A New view of the magnitude of human personality, its dimensions and resources*. New York: McGraw-Hill, 1963. Then, *At a Journal Workshop: The basic text and guide for using the Intensive Journal*. New York: Dialogue House Library, 1975. Then, *Three Cycles of Process Meditation: The Well and the Cathedral; The Star/Cross; The White Robed Monk*. New York: Dialogue House Library, 1972. Lastly, *Jung's Psychology and its Social Meaning*. New York: Doubleday, 1973.

3. See my *The Secular Magi: Marx, Freud and Nietzsche on Religion*. New York: Pilgrim, 1986. Chapter IV gives a short account of Freud's technique of infecting the patient with his own neurosis to create a crisis which might precipitate growth in the patient.

4. Kenneth Burke, *A Grammar of Motives*. Berkeley Calif.: University of California Press, 1969.

5. William F. Lynch, S.J., "Theology and the Imagination", in "Thought", pp. 61-86, passim.

6. The September, 1976 edition [Vol. 11, no. 3] of "Zygon" -- a journal of religion and science -- is devoted to genetic and cultural evolution. Though no evidence is determinative, the hypothesis that both individual [genetic] and cultural [evolutionary] traits have been developed offers rich possibilities. This means that my intuition that certain groups develop

certain traits, both positive and negative, along certain lines may be empirically grounded. By this, I mean that different people value certain things and scotch out of their purview that which threatens them as individuals and groups. This shapes people both genetically and culturally, the latter in the development of cultural traits. So, it may be a possible explanation for the differing ways we do theology in the various religions and even within them, as with Catholics and Protestants. This means that one will find certain things in a religion, even one's own, and miss other salient features. Not to use one's interiority in the name of objectivity is to fail to be oneself epistemologically and psychologically. Not to be challenged by the real in others is to fail to grow epistemologically, psychologically and theologically.

_____. *The Reshaping of Catholicism: Current Challenges in the Theology of the Church.*

Eliade, Mircea. *Cosmos and History: The Myth of the Eternal Return.* New York: Harper, 1959.

_____. *The Sacred and Profane: The Nature of Religion.* New York: Harper, 1961.

_____. *Patterns in Comparative Religion.* Trans. by Rosemary Sheed. New York: World Publishing Co., 1963.

_____. *The Quest.* Chicago: University of Chicago Press, 1969.

Farley, Edward. *Ecclesial Reflection: An Anatomy of Theological Method.* Philadelphia: Fortress Press, 1982.

Gadamer, Hans-Georg. *Truth and Method.* New York: Seabury, 1975.

Goleman, Daniel. *Vital Lies, Simple Truths.* New York: Simon and Schuster, 1985.

Halpern, Baruch. *The First Historians: The Hebrew Bible and History.* San Francisco: Harper & Row, 1988.

Hug, James E., S.J., editor. *Tracing the Spirit: Communities, Social Action, and Theological Reflection.* Woodstock Theological Center. New York: Paulist Press, 1983.

Keirsey, David, and Bates, Marilyn. *Please Understand Me: An Essay on Temperament Styles.* Del Mar, Ca.: Prometheus Nemesis Books, 1978.

Kristensen, W. Brede. *The Meaning of Religion, Lectures in the Phenomenology of Religion.* Trans. by John B. Carman. The Hague: M. Nijhoff, 1960.

Kuhn, Thomas S. *The Structure of Scientific Revolutions.* Chicago: U. of Chicago Press, 2nd. ed., 1970.

Langer, Susanne K. *Philosophy in a New Key, A Study in the Symbolism of Reason, Rite, and Art.* New York: Mentor, 1951.

Lindbeck, George, A. *The Future of Roman Catholic Theology.* Philadelphia: Fortress Press, 1969.

_____. *The Nature of Doctrine: Religion and Theology in a Postliberal Age.* Philadelphia: Westminster Press, 1985.

Lonergan, Bernard, S.J. *Insight: A Study of Human Understanding.*

_____. *Method in Theology.* New York: Herder and Herder, 1972.

Lynch, William F., S.J.. *Christ and Prometheus: A New Image of the Secular.* South Bend: Notre Dame U. Press, 1978.

_____. *Images of Faith: An Exploration of the Ironic Imagination.* Notre Dame: University of Notre Dame Press, 1973.

Naranjo, Claudio, and Ornstein, Robert E. *On the Psychology of Meditation.* New York: the Viking Press, 1971.

Newell, William Lloyd. *Struggle and Submission: R.C. Zaehner on Mysticisms.* Washington: University Press of America, 198

_____. *The Secular Magi: Marx, Freud and Nietzsche on Religion.* New York: The Pilgrim Press, 1986.

Nishitani, Keiji. *Religion and Nothingness.* Trans. with an Introduction by Jan Van Bragt. Berkeley: U. of California Press, 1983.

O'Leary, Joseph S. *Questioning Back: the overcoming of metaphysics in Christian Tradition.* Minneapolis: Winston-Seabury, 1985.

Palmer, Helen. *The Enneagram: Understanding Yourself and the Others in Your Life.* San Francisco: Harper & Row, 1988.

Pelikan, Jaroslav. *Jesus Through the Centuries: his place in the history of culture.* New York: Harper & Row, 1985.

Progoff, Ira. *Depth Psychology an Modern Man: A new view of the magnitude of human personality, its dimensions and resources.*   New York: McGraw-Hill, 1973.

136

_____. *Jung, Synchronicity and Human Destiny: Non-Causal Dimensions of Human Experience.* New York: Julian Press, 1973.

_____.*At a Journal Workshop: the basic text and guide for using the Intensive Journal.* New York: Dialogue House, 1975.

_____. *Jung's Psychology and Its Social Meaning.* New York: Doubleday, 1973.

_____. *Three Cycles of Process Meditation: The Well and the Cathedral, The Star/Cross, The White Robed Monk.* New York: Dialogue House, 1972.

_____.*The Symbolic and the Real: A New Psychological Approach to the Fuller Experience of Personal Existence.* New York: McGraw-Hill, 1973.

Rahner, Karl, S.J. *Theological Investigations,* especially Vol. 4, *More Recent Writings.* London: Darton, Longman and Todd, 1974.

_____.*The Foundations of Christian Faith. An Introduction to the Idea of Christianity.* Trans. by William V. Dyche. New York: Seabury, 1978.

Ricoeur, Paul. *The Symbolism of Evil.* Trans. by Emerson Buchanan. Boston: Beacon Press, 1967.

_____. *The Conflict of Interpretations: Essays in Hermeneutics.* Evanston, Il.: Northwestern University Press, 1974.

_____.*Freud and Philosophy: An essay on Interpretation.* Trans. by Denis Savage. New Haven: Yale University Press, 1977.

Rike, Jennifer. *Being and Mystery: analogy and its linguistic implications in the thought of Karl Rahner.* An unpublished dissertation from the U. of Chicago, 1986.

Smith, Huston. *The Religions of Man.* New York: Harper & Row, 1958.

Smith, Wilfred Cantwell. *Faith and Belief.* Princeton: Princeton University Press, 1979.

_____. *Towards a World Theology, Faith and the Comparative History of Religion*. Philadelphia: Westminster, 1981.

Stcherbatski, T. *The Conception of Buddhist Nirvana*. Leningrad, 1927.

Streng, Frederick. *Emptiness, A Study in Religious Meaning*. Nashville: Abingdon Press, 1968.

Suzuki, D.T. *Essays in Zen Buddhism*. First Series. New York: Grove Press, 1961.

_____. *On Indian Mahayana Buddhism*. Ed. with an Intro. by E.Conze. New York: Harper Torchbooks, 1968

Tracy, David. *The Analogical Imagination: Christian theology and the culture of pluralism*. New York: Crossroad, 1981.

_____. *Plurality and Ambiguity: Hermeneutics, Religion, Hope*. San Francisco: Harper & Row, 1987.

Von Franz, Marie Louise and Hillman, James. *Lectures on Jung's Typology*. Zurich: Spring Publications, 1971.

Waldenfels, Hans. *Kontextuelle Fundamental-theologie.* Paderborn: Ferdinand Schoeningh, 1985.

_____. *Absolute Nothingness: Foundations for a Buddhist-Christian Dialogue*. Trans. by J.W. Heisig. New York: Paulist, 1980.

Welbon, Guy R. *The Buddhist Nirvana and its Western Interpreters*. Chicago: University of Chicago Press, 1968; a Ph.D. thesis, unpublished.

Wilson, Colin. *Poetry and Mysticism*. San Francisco: City Light Press, 1970.

Zaehner, R.C. *The Bhagavad Gita, With a Commentary Based on the Original Sources*. Oxford: Oxford Press, 1969.

Zukav, Gary. *The Dancing Wu Li Masters. An Overview of the New Physics*. New York: William Morrow, 1979.